GRAFT

Steven Berkoff

GRAFT

TALES OF AN ACTOR

OBERON BOOKS
LONDON

First published in 1998 by Oberon Books
(incorporating Absolute Classics),
521 Caledonian Rd, London N7 9RH.

Tel: 0171 607 3637
Fax: 0171 607 3629
e-mail: oberon.books@btinternet.com

British Library Cataloguing-in-Publication Data. A catalogue record for this book is available from the British Library.

ISBN 1 84002 040 7

Cover photograph: Robin Barton

Cover design: Andrzej Klimowski

Typography: Richard Doust

Printed in Great Britain by Arrowhead Books Ltd, Reading.

For Clara

"...and cease to fume at destiny by ever grumbling at today or lamenting tomorrow."

Marcus Aurelius

STEVEN BERKOFF

Widely known as an actor, director and playwright, Steven Berkoff is one of the leading British exponents of modern theatre with a taste for stark contrasts and disturbing juxtapositions. His original and outrageous play, *East*, combined Shakespearean grandeur and cockney rhyming slang to riotous effect. Adaptations include Kafka's *Metamorphosis* and *The Trial*, Oscar Wilde's *Salome* and further stage plays such as *Greek* and *Kvetch* all performed throughout the world, earning him an international following.

CONTENTS

AUDITION

Audition

Yes, it was the day of reckoning. The moment of truth. The audition for a grant at the local Town Hall where a group of sedate ladies and gentlemen sat behind a large desk while you sweated and writhed in the throes of thespian passion. One Shakespeare piece was expected, and one modern, so on the deliverance and wit of your performance that day, lay your entire future as a member of that noble art. However, Harry was brimming with the confidence that a year of thrice weekly sessions at his local Working Men's Institute had given him. Those evening classes had kept the flame of his ambition burning when, after a day engaged in the vile servitude of a menswear shop (the lower end of the trade), he would dive into the Tube with the enthusiasm of an escaping convict. A blunted education at a grim Hackney school had trained him for nothing more demanding, but Harry was to change all that. Leaping up the escalator a yard at a time, he arrived at the sacred area of learning, spun down the corridor, senses on high alert, and already sucking in the smell of study, sweat and classroom polish, burst into the room, took a deep breath and filled his lungs with the aura of literature, voice and gesture. Yes, he was home!

Throughout the year had he not diligently attended his classes – sitting and absorbing, as sand absorbs the sea, as bread absorbs gravy? He drank at the rivers of wisdom and forgot about the belittling, humiliating and soul destroying work he was obliged to do, but blessed it as well for now his passion, his fury, his desire, his thirst was that much greater by contrast, his need to compensate that much more intense. And so, perhaps it was destined.

He would arrive and thrust himself into the maelstrom of bodies in the canteen, fuelling himself with hot, weak tea and cheese and chutney sandwiches; absorb the intense buzz in the room from the other spirits whose thirst, lack of earlier opportunities, and deep frustration had led them, like a herd of wildebeest, to lap at the great lake of knowledge that the Institute provided. For it was not only drama that the Institute offered, but a thousand other subjects in the arts – languages, history, archaeology, philosophy, economics, still-life painting, needlework, classical Greek, opera appreciation, playwriting, music, dance – a never-ending mosaic of mankind's fascinating quest to chart every element of its infinite being. Drama for Harry was not, as it was for many, merely a hobby, a desire to improve oneself and discover ways and means of heightening an unadventurous life. For Harry this was to be the means whereby the oaken laurel might one day be placed on his head.

After the tea came the work, the texts to be performed for the long suffering teachers who were professional practitioners of their arts, eking out an existence in the repertory theatre with part-time work. It was at least constant, and spared them the corrosive torments of unemployment. So, Harry would get up and perform in front of the class. These weekly sessions were his Rubicon, and there he sat happily absorbing the atmosphere of chalky classrooms, wax polish and tomato soup smells wafting up from the canteen, mixing together to produce that special aroma of memory.

It was there that he saw a young woman, the like of which he had never before encountered; thick, teeming, auburn hair tumbled down her round, pale face from which two large, grey eyes stared out with fascination and reminded Harry of a big, furry Persian cat. Only here could he have seen such a pre-Raphaelite beauty like Rosemary, who was born never to say the vulgar 'rrrr', but pwonounced everything that had the rude growl of the 'r' as a more pliant 'wa.' Wosemawee was charming beyond all imagination and wore black, lacy stockings under her voluminous skirts. She was more beautiful than anything Harry had laid eyes on up to then, elegantly, classically, intelligently beautiful. Harry surmised this was an aesthetic quality that could only be formed from what lay within, that was illumined by the special glow that sparkled her eyes. Her parchmenty skin was veiled in a thinnish make-up, giving her an aura of faded gentility that you would find in the steaming, poetic landscape of a Tennessee Williams play. Harry saw immediately that she and he were destined to do a scene from *A Streetcar Named Desire* together in the class. They did, in future months, work on that famous scene together, and now... Rosemary, Wosemawee, where are you? Do you live and breathe, my love? Are you thriving somewhere with grown-up children? You were the first and most exquisite creature I ever saw and seemed to materialise from *Alice in Wonderland.*

So, in front of her and the class, Harry would get up and perform, as they all did – young unseasoned meat, undercooked and without taste. Nevertheless, each week one ransacked the world of drama as if raiding an old clothes store, trying on what suited. It was all there to bring out something of you that you wished to show, or give, or express, and why was it that you could only reveal yourself through the words of others, as if the writer gave you permission to show who you were. For some it was drink that allowed them to loosen the doors to their soul, but for the actor it was words. And if the words were right, you felt you were more alive as they drew the essence out of you. The teacher would often suggest a speech based on his observation of his uninformed student. Harry started with Launcelot Gobbo, from *The Merchant of Venice*, Shylock's pathetic, comic servant (and yes, the class giggled) and then had a go at Richard III, when the teacher advised Richard II, but, in the full bloom of ignorance, felt that it was at least numerically close. Then, one session, he performed one of the sons in *Death of a Salesman* – the speech where the son steals a pen from the desk of the man he has come to see for a job, because he has to take something. So he has the pen in his hand, and what a curious observation to tell his father, that he has thieved the boss's pen from his desk. Did Arthur do that at one time in his life? Of course he did, for this kind of observation comes from your own experience; that horrible time when you were a fluctuating thing. And did Harry not do the very same thing, which shamed him, reverting to that small, needy, desperate childhood? You feel dead, empty, powerless, impotent and you approach everyone like a beggar and then take something to inflict a tiny wound.

Harry liked doing the American plays since their spirit spoke to him more and he could identify with their problems. The English were not as real, or were just symbols to hang a polemic on, a coat-hanger for a theory, a few pithy sentences, some ideological sausage minced from many different animals with a lot of indigestible gristle – and Osborne was meant to have changed all that. Here was a spitting cauldron spouting working class, educated, bolshy language, but it still felt like coat-hanger language. In the American plays you recognised the people, and so Harry looked at Clifford Odets, Tennessee Williams, Eugene O'Neill, William Saroyan – hardly any British, with the exception of Shakespeare whose characters felt completely real again – Hamlet, Hotspur, Gobbo.

So the year crept on with its terms and breaks, then the welcoming back, the new faces, while the old felt like true and trusted friends; all of them getting up week after week to perform their speeches, and the class being asked its opinion.

After a time, Harry became more sartorially aware and adapted himself after work to the current trend, the 'French' look, wearing black roll-neck sweaters, drainpipe trousers and black cap. A cynic in the canteen felt inspired to comment, "You know, Harry, I saw three chaps outside Joe Lyons (tea-shops, alas, now extinct) looking just like you... ha... ha!" Quick as a flash Harry responded with, "That's funny, because I saw fifty chaps inside Joe Lyons looking just like *you*..."

So Harry remembered those nuggets as the year drew to its close. In between Rosemary and Richard were grated cheese sandwiches and tea and the institutional aroma that stayed in one's clothes; the coffee bars (as they were called) where they would gather after the class like crows sitting around a small table, digging their spoons into the hardened granules of brown sugar, sipping frothy cappuccino served in glass cups and furiously discussing Bertolt Brecht. The Institute was a sanctuary, a home, a cradle of the dramatic arts where he sucked furiously on the nipple of culture. Out of the crowd some would make the leap across the chasm and become professionals, but for most, it was a place to go, a thing to flirt with but never marry, and for many it was just a chance to escape loneliness and perhaps meet someone. Harry, on the other hand, was determined to make that leap, cockily waving at the others after he had crossed that gulf, and then watching them looking a little wistful as they went back for another year of classes – the Chekhovs, Juliets and Romeos and Lady Macbeths, sleepwalking, reading letters, seeing invisible daggers...

Harry chose that cool spring morning to do his two pieces – one classic, one modern. Naïvely, he had chosen Richard III and the Gentleman Caller from *The Glass Menagerie* by Tennessee Williams... "You know what I judge to be the trouble with you, Laura? Inferiority complex!"

When the application form from the drama board arrived to be filled out, the heart sank: Where were you educated? How many 'A' or 'O' levels, degrees, awards? ... "Oh, my prophetic soul, what could I say?" Harry anguished inside the deep confines of his being. For days he stared at the open form, its neat folds still holding the pristine top and bottom away from the table, and wondered about lying and inventing some minor awards, anxiously debating with himself the chances of his 'facts' being checked. But, as is nearly always the case, the sweating over a decision burns away the adipose tissue and one is left with a braver, cleaner core, i.e., come clean and tell the truth. If he confessed and scraped at the very bottom of the barrel of revelations right to its mouldy base, the very candour of the confession, its utter nakedness, might make a small pathway to their hearts, for he had, in their minds, no merits to recommend him. No 'levels' of any kind. His fifteenth birthday had not even quite struck before he was shunted out of a school that had little time for him or interest in his future. An indifferent family life had left him to mix with assorted low-lifes and potential delinquents, which eventually led him before a strict magistrate who had no hesitation in using Harry as a guinea pig for a new and highly experimental 'detention centre' with an ultra-rigorous regime. This was meant to act as a 'shock to the system' and prevent you ever dreaming of committing antisocial acts again. To cap it all, his school, standing like a bleak prison in a damp Hackney, had not trained him in any way. The low demands of the work and the crude, unskilled and boring tasks he was made to do, compelled Harry to jump from job to job, just for the relief of leaving one and having a few days off before starting another. So between the ages of fifteen and twenty, when he applied for a grant to put his boat on some kind of course on the choppy seas of life, he estimated roughly that he had worked for no less than SIXTY employers!! Ha ha ha ha ha ha! "No, I did not go to uni and decide, after three heavily subsidised years, that I wanted two more subsidised years." Harry had grafted in every squalid, ordinary, ugly, pathetic, time-wasting, boring, soul destroying, pointless, agonising, humiliating job – but not all – not quite all, but most. Now, in the sweet, soupy smell of education, of culture, of heart, of sensitivity, of drama and of Wosemawee, Harry had at last found the balm, the very ointment for the soul... And here, at last, at long last, after thousands of deadening hours standing in shops, in warehouses, in purgatory, after all those hours of rotting life-denial, he now had the chance to taste the succulent joys of studying, of being a full-time student.

Harry poured his truth onto the form and left nothing out. Shortly after, he received a notification that he had been accepted as a candidate for an audition. It was a crisp morning when Harry arrived and, as he was early, he practised his lines and stared into a fast flowing Thames. Two weeks later Harry received, at the council tower block where he lived somehow in the sky, a letter confirming his acceptance as the recipient of a grant. They would pay not only his grant, but award him a small living income as well. The beginning had arrived. He turned up nervously for the first day of the new term as a full-time student. The past was buried.

FREE ASSOCIATE

Free Associate

"Whatever comes into your head..." said the teacher, encouraging the young group of actors to improvise. "Unleash the ferocity of human imagination which, like coal, is the condensed matter of experience, and are you ready, children, to mine it, dig it out and heat your art with it, are you?" Mr. Lind was rather fond of using such emphatic metaphors, since being a native of Germany, English was a second tongue that seemed to allow him to play with imagery as if to compensate for his narrower vocabulary. "Are you ready? What surprises will you excavate – diamonds or stones? Stones you can gather on the surface, but diamonds are locked in hard clay and need effort and perseverance. However, start with pebbles and work down. Harry, you begin..."

Harry felt a cold wave of shock go through him. A lightning stroke. A slap. He could not believe that he would be chosen to begin their weekly impro class for one simple reason – he was never that good. He couldn't get beneath the surface of his mind where the treasures lay, but scurried around on top like a scared rabbit without a burrow, constantly aware of the faces examining him. And now it was the same, as his body was raked by their searchlights and each one in the room fixed on a different part of his being – some on his jeans, others on his shoes, his hair, the slight shine now appearing on his face, his sweater that somehow found itself half in and half out of his waist, his stance, his awkward grin of mock humiliation that each contender feels obliged to wear as a token, a kind of 'forgive me' in advance. But the students were relieved – at least they had time to think of their own impros and get rid of him first. Harry was not one of US. He chattered amiably enough in the institute canteen while chewing on his favourite cheese and chutney sandwiches, but never really joined in their class post-mortems in the pub. These were gatherings of the serious ones, whose ambitions had already in their wild and fevered imaginations been granted. Now Harry sat in the centre of the room and felt as if everything about him was emphasised beyond belief. The class were no longer colleagues but an unsympathetic jury taking him apart, judging him. His crime was merely being Harry, but that was enough for there is always identification, even if it is of the 'thank God I am not he' kind. There must be some way in which the watcher feels connected, feels empathy and therefore hostility. They must detect some part of themselves in him, and if mankind seek to identify with heroes for strength, they also fear drawing weakness from victims, since all people fear the weakness in themselves. Harry is the enemy, however even this wretch might, with some wit and skill hitherto only hinted at, suck the oxygen of approval out of the class, and they might laugh or even clap.

At that moment Harry could feel their contempt like a ray of heat. Contempt is also a form of fear that one day you will step on the slippery slope, irrevocably sliding down, and crash into that thing at the bottom, where Harry and all the other rejects lay. So, you must avoid what you fear and not sit with him, if possible, in the canteen, but rather join the bright and the future darlings. In Harry is what you both loathe and fear. In him you see the worst part of yourself, be it even a fraction, a splinter, an infinitely small particle of yourself, that is enough. These people are to be avoided for fear of contamination by association.

Yes, Harry often found himself alone at the canteen table, unless there was an overflow from the other tables. As the students took their mugs of tea and rolls from the self-service bar their eyes would scan the room, like seasoned hikers avoiding the crags and bogs. Of course, Harry was regarded as the bog. On the lively tables the young neophytes would be examining and criticising performances that came short of their pompous self-esteem, upbraiding well-known actors with the swollen arrogance of youth.

The centre of attention was a young man called Neil. With his thick mane of hair tumbling over one eye and his laconic North country twang that gave much of what he said an air of cynical working class authority, he was surrounded by giggling, admiring girls. Harry watched as the girls chortled loudly, then in an odd action he turned around to see if others in the canteen were observing their exuberant jollity. He munched his sandwich and thought how classes are the great leveller. No matter how clever, how handsome, how popular with the girls or how unfriendly you are, in the end what counts is what you do when you're out there. He turned his head casually to scan the buzzing heads in the room and watched each table full of excited students ready to fill their minds with the subject of their choice. Harry went back to nibbling his sandwich and drinking his cup of sweet tea and found himself joined by another classroom outsider, an older man who, suddenly taken with the idea of studying drama, fancied himself as a kind of clown and was over-enthusiastic about everything with that boyish exhilaration of the newly converted. Harry was glad of the natter but couldn't fail to see how he had been sought out by the class idiot, as if the die was cast and the herd had exiled him along with the rejects.

Now he sat alone in the middle of a circle of stares. He could see in their unenvying eyes that they wished him to get on with it and get it over with so that Neil could show his superior mettle. He felt their collective electric current running up and down his body, making assessments and strengthening themselves on the evaluations thereof. His jeans were a trifle too baggy. The back pocket had been torn off, leaving a pale blue square. His plimsolls looked much grimier here than outside and his hair was sticking to his damp forehead. Everything was in battle with everything else. Chaos. He didn't normally look at the class in such situations. He tried to defocus or look for a gap in the chairs, but today the class was full and he couldn't help but see them looking at him. Harry tried to be absent. Someone else would be this heaving mass of flesh, blood and bone while Harry was on automatic, but he couldn't escape from his fleshly prison. They looked, but not with such hostility as he had imagined they might – more quizzically, questioning and waiting. They looked as they did in the canteen, still grouped together as they were around the table. One or two of the leading lights had taken opposite sides of the classroom, to divide territory so to speak, and were surrounded by their acolytes.

The improvisations were started by Mr. Lind arbitrarily pointing a finger at you and you were obliged to get up and do it. So you waited, heart thumping in anticipation, but often the session hadn't time for everyone so you were spared the stocks but also left curiously empty, not having purged yourself. Last week's impros had ended with Neil holding the class in the palm of his hand like a stand-up comic. Everybody shrieked at the wit, the drollness and the easy invention, but they also laughed because they knew Neil and were familiar with his flip Scouse arrogance and acidic barbs. Even as he sauntered into the middle of the room, the chums were already geared to respond and smiled in expectation.

But now Harry turns up and is asked by Mr. Lind to dig deeper and "find something inside you that you didn't know you had." Although Harry knew this was an exhortation to the class, it felt as if it was aimed at him as the one to begin. Or was he saying that Neil, the handsome, the satiric, with his thick quiff of bouncing boyish hair, so admired by the girls for being easy and humorous, was only digging for cheap ore, common metal and not diamonds? Or was he referring to Harry's own hitherto painful struggles to exhibit himself to a public he would have gladly hidden from? While Mr Lind continued his lecture Harry sat there sheepishly, grinned tightly and tried to appear casual by thrusting his hands into the pockets of his jeans.

"OK Harry... PREPARATION..."

Mr. Lind liked these one-word titles for his improvisations. The simpler they were, the more the beast of imagination would leap at it, roaring and gnashing its teeth. Harry's beast, however, was nervously pounding its cage like a sick old cat. This was the impro that had not been completed by everyone last week, and Mr. Lind did like everyone to have a go before he changed the lesson. With impros, as each student performs, he or she reduces the amount of available material, and one can almost see a student wince as the improviser plunges into an area the untried performer had planned for himself; hence the teacher's admonition to dig deep. Neil, of course, had scored heavily with his impro, preparing to go to work; waking late, tripping over his pants (all mimed of course), cutting himself shaving, knocking over a teapot, scalding himself, changing his wet pants, looking for his keys, feeding the cat, cutting his finger on the tin, looking for an elastoplast... He just kept going as one idea seeded the next, a veritable Monsieur Hulot going from one catastrophe to another.

Harry's heart thumped. It was a deliberate humiliation to make him follow that comedian. He didn't have a thought or an idea in his head, but he had thought of doing 'getting up' until Neil completely ransacked the subject. Now his brain was racing between the embarrassment of being there in the middle of the room as a not very popular being and the lead balloon attached to his imagination. Harry felt that it was unfair that Neil had the advantage of being 'popular,' and so it followed that he would be more relaxed in facing people in whose affections he was safe and protected. Harry could see the eyes of the other students, who hadn't yet exposed their impros, starting to foresee their own scenarios, getting nervous at the prospect... chewing their jaws in anticipation as they inwardly presented their own scripts. Harry got up from the plywood institutional chair with nothing in his head and hoped that at the last second would come a reprieve from the imagination – but NOTHING. A 'surgeon' had already been done very funnily as the actor mimed the bizarre assortment of things that materialised from within the belly; a girl did a lover preparing herself; someone did a thief about to break into a house. And so the word 'preparation' covered a vast array of possibilities. "OK, Harry, now let's see your *preparation...*" and Mr. Lind went to his chair.

Harry was alone as never before in his life, in the middle of a roomful of eyes peeling him down like paint stripper. He closed his own for a second as though he could project some image onto the inside of his eyelids by shutting out the distraction of the outer world. A slow anger was beginning to rise and, mimicking a microbe or antibody, was chewing up the fear. Yet, while Harry still had no idea, he did appear to possess a feeling, and it was this feeling, this new anger, that was to inspire his impro... What he did then was so bizarre, horrible, obscene and wicked that class talked about it for weeks to come. Something changed in the community. When Harry sat alone in the canteen he found that others joined his table and solicited his opinion on a new play or film that had recently opened and warmed themselves by his presence. But Harry knew that these were fair-weather friends whose loyalty he could not trust. However, he let out a deep sigh of satisfaction, as if he at last recognised his new worth and couldn't help but relish it.

REP

Rep

It was the first day and everyone gathered around for the reading. They wandered into the room from the four corners of England, some from London, the provinces and some from other reps. This group of actors would now unite and be part of each other's lives, hopes and destinies for the next two months. Initially, Harry thought the two small roles assigned to him weren't too bad; not plum parts but serviceable enough to make something of, to create a small but respectable impact. He had already torn through the play and pounced on his lines, going over and over them so as to be prepared for the reading. Now, as everyone sat around and acted out their lines, he was uncomfortably aware how long he had to wait before he spoke. Then hardly had he got his few words out before he was consigned to long stretches of silently listening to others feasting on the language and on their characters, warming into their roles. He sat waiting for the train to stop at his station when he could once again join it for a few more pathetic moments before being set down again in the wastelands. When you are not there in a play you no longer have a life, and so he sat and watched the others laughing at some not so very funny dialogue, laughing in that way of support and camaraderie, while he found it more and more like an arrow pointing once more to his isolation.

His was a peripheral character, one of those linking parts that has a function only to service and highlight the roles of others, reacting to events, a small boat tossing on the ocean of others' endeavours. He did, however, have one speech as a kind of barker at a fair, a device that was used to comment on the events of the plot. The speech couldn't have lasted more than three minutes in a play which droned on for three hours. He had been working on it hoping to use it to show off his declamatory and physical skills. Once the play was on and when it came to his link in the great chain of events, the audience would see only him, and who was to know how long his role would last, maybe three minutes and maybe an hour... a day? How do we know? He knows, but the audience do not, and so, for those three minutes, he has the audience in his power to do with them as he wishes, but audiences are not dumb beasts who cannot anticipate the future. No, they have the mysterious sense that all knowledge is finite and unconsciously allocate only small crumbs of attention to the minor characters, saving themselves for the stars with whom they identify. If the small character outstays his welcome, the audience becomes restless and turns away, not wishing to spend their lives with people of NO CONSEQUENCE.

Now all the actors are gathered round the long table giggling at the *double entendres*, smiling at each other as they mutually enjoyed the witty ripostes, taking in the others when not immediately engaged, making quick and superficial assessments, and of course, checking out the females without whose soft, sensual, understanding, compassionate, friendly, open company, rep would indeed be dull. So the female in rep, heavily outnumbered by the men, is usually far rarer and of greater value than she would be in the more evenly balanced demography of a city. Here they are as gold dust, and you must be quick to stake your claim lest you finish your performance with little job satisfaction and face the long, yawning abyss of night with a ghastly English provincial town staring you blankly in the face. Then the walk back to your cold, bloodless, provincial digs and the solace of unconsciousness which takes forever to come; when mercifully it does, you have only the vast aching emptiness of a grey day forming the backdrop to hell to look forward to and hope there is a decent movie to go to in the afternoon. There weren't many women in the play and the ones that were there tended to be 'character bags', saucy middle-aged hags who dig their elbows into your ribs and guffaw loudly. "Not much talent here," thought Harry but still, as every actor knows, there is the backstage to scour – the usherettes, bar staff, wardrobe etc., and for a keen eye and nose, no stone will be left unturned.

The group of actors involved in the sub-plot, including Harry, were shunted together to make it easier for the director to identify them. After the reading they were already coalescing as a team and thinking out 'business' for each other, getting very involved and making excitable gestures. Harry was on the periphery even of this, but at least had his three minute speech as the fairground barker, although when he read it through it seemed more like two minutes. The leading actor was a handsome youth, too young by far for the role, but had been picked as someone to watch and was being 'groomed!' He had been seen at Cambridge and had already played in some top division reps. No summer season for him, oh no! No working behind the bar in smelly pubs when things were quiet and when you wondered if you would ever work again! The 'star' had a friendly disposition and gave his smile to everyone, as if he wished in some way to compensate the rest of us for taking the biggest role and hoped not to be thought of too badly for it. He had strolled in for the reading after the others, but not deliberately, since the other actors were all here rather early, keen to be quit of their rotten digs. Of course in those days we had to find them ourselves by examining the stage-doorman's well-thumbed digs list.

Harry had a small bedsitter on the edge of town which comprised a single bed covered with a candlewick spread, a mouldy, chilly carpet and a two-bar, electric fire which seemed only to last a couple of hours before you were scurrying to the corner pub to change more pounds into the silver coins it gobbled so ravenously before shitting them out into the landlady's rapacious fist. None of the other actors were staying there because keen Harry had arrived early the day before and had not teamed up with anyone; nor in fact did he know any of them. He wondered if the others stayed in groups or paired up?

So, on the day of the reading Harry got down to the theatre early and hung about with that air of high expectancy everyone has on the first day. He found a cheap workman's café for breakfast and then drifted round the theatre, staring at photographs of past productions. The photographs always looked somehow intense and full of life, but he knew that photographers had their way of selecting, printing and making something dull look like a major event in theatre history.

Harry was ever early, as far as he could recall. Even as a child there was a feverish anticipation of what the day could bring in the way of exciting and fathomless mysteries. Upon waking he would leap out of bed and explore this amazing world, starting with the world of the senses as he cooked his own breakfast, while ma and pa still lay in the land of peace and were reluctant to leave it. The world they occupied was fraught with care and as different to the world of young Harry as living on another planet. He went to the never-to-be-missed Saturday morning cinema, a ritual that was as much a part of his life as all his other rituals that were defined by seasons or custom. The cinema opened at 9am, but his solitary figure found it intensely satisfying to be there before anyone else. He could be seen standing there alone at 8am and enjoying the sensation of the queue growing behind him. He recalled one occasion when he arrived as usual at the ungodly hour and the queue had formed as usual behind him, but it was unruly that morning. A light rain had made them push and shove. The queue was getting broader, rather than longer, and since he was quite small, he was pushed to the edge, still in front, but not for long. Eventually, the commissionaire broke the queue into two lines, thinning out the tangle. Harry was now at the front of the second queue, but when the box office opened, as luck would have it, the first queue was served; and that line had now grown longer, since the canny ones who had been at the end of the second line had broken off and joined the first. So Harry was left near the end! Before long, the commissionaire came out to announce that the house was full and Harry, who had so carefully prepared for that morning's ritual, was without a goal and drifted back home.

Exported out of his digs, waiting – eating a slow breakfast over a newspaper, all this was in keeping with his earlier feelings of waking up full of optimism that was sourly rewarded. He felt these familiar sensations of isolation and drift as if this was his due; a mild rebuke for existing. When the family of man sat round the table to feast on the drama, it didn't seem odd that they gathered in twos and threes; the actors knew each other from some rep or drama school; and as Harry felt in some sense that he was sending himself to Coventry, there was little need, it seemed, to make an effort beyond politeness to gain anyone's intimacy or interest. The other actors, innocently unaware of the storms going on beneath the calm mask, interpreted his manner as aloofness or sour grapes... Everybody, in one way or another, has their own inner storms to contend with. Nevertheless they try to set sail rather than sulk in the harbour of their various griefs. But in this case, having been allocated one of the smallest parts in the play was tantamount to a public declaration that his talents were the least respected by the director and his self-isolation was partly induced by the arrow of shame pointing directly to him.

"All actors are part of the one show so why should I feel not even worthy of their company?" he pondered. "After all, these were good working actors who like to imbibe after a show and enjoy a good natter, play darts in the green room and watch football between the matinée and evening on the telly." It was ever thus. Did they not laugh at Kean, the great nineteenth century tragedian, but of course Kean had the last laugh as 'they' faded into dusty obscurity. Harry sucked at these venomous little thoughts like they were boiled sweets, filling his mind with comforting flavours. The pack, he thought, seek out like-minded souls anyway, wishing to extract the best possible time out of this experience without having to adjust to the difficult or curious. The rehearsals were long and tedious since the play was a pile of old cobblers and had never been performed for the good reason that it stank of fusty history, unredeemed by any strong dramatic sense. It was one of those rediscovered classics allegedly penned in part by Shakespeare in league with others. Yes, it was a great forgettable yawn. The leading actor made the most of his youthful experience and sensitivity while the secondary players did a good job and were workmanlike. The sub-group, of which Harry was one, attacked their parts like ravenous dogs wagging their stumpy little tails with glee.

At 5pm the rehearsals ended and then came a long, long wait until the next day. Unlike some of the actors in the 'rep', he was not performing in the other plays but was hired only to swell the company for the season's 'classic.' He would be discarded at the end since the rep could not afford to keep such a large group all year round. The actors drifted off to their digs or ganged up to have a group nosh. Harry lingered around the theatre, exulted to be free for the first five minutes until, like his morning awakening, his energy would just drift into space finding no reciprocal force to link with it. Like being in a muddy stream of life that drifted around the theatre, he let the current take him first to the bar, hoping there to strike up a chat with another actor who had splintered off from the group. Yes, there was one other who seemed to have been rejected from the team as not being altogether worthy or interesting enough. Another reject. So, perhaps he could collect a few of them. John was intensely tedious and full of himself, but it was better than nothing. Then perhaps a stroll to the Chinese restaurant and a visit to the current show, which was rather good and starred again the young actor, thoroughly enjoying himself in a role that suited his youth, and that was a good night, but after? Who can even remember the days of pain and emptiness? The digs; a long read in bed and an attempt to sleep; an early rise; the same dreary, bleary, dull, ghastly walk up the high street past symbols everywhere of death – square life, insurance building, squalid burger-bars where grim-eyed humans sat and stared lifelessly out of the window and the familiar landmarks of Britain – Boots the Chemist, a Woolworths, a Sainsburys and a post office and then a pub on the corner of the street leading to the theatre.

He wandered into the theatre's coffee bar and waited for the actors to drift in for rehearsal. Of course, John was the first and they exchanged meagre scraps of info on discoveries made since the previous night, which amounted to nothing more nourishing than lurid descriptions of their respective digs. However, the reason he was here was to be tested, and he had spent time polishing his small soliloquy of the fairground barker who summons up the public, and was determined to create a moment... to arrest the ear and eye of the audience with this scrap of material. Yes, his small flag would nevertheless ripple in the wind of his inspiration and all would see it. He was determined to make it a powerful piece of declamation, gestural, physical, eye catching, since this is how his 'barker' must be in order to capture a sullen and indifferent crowd.

The rehearsal droned on. One of the actors, who had been given, in preference to Harry, the meatier of the small roles of a political agitator, was hopeless. He could not match the words to the actions and his movements were stiff and awkward and Harry eyed him hungrily and also angrily for having the plum part and being so obviously unable to digest it. All the small parts then got stuck into a 'street scene,' a terrible bore resembling one of those folksy 'ye olde yokels' street scenes with everyone being rural and bumpkin. The day ground itself down like coffee – an extremely bitter one – and was, in the end, without form and void, and the evening tightened itself around Harry like a noose. It was becoming unbearable, intolerable, unspeakable, inexorable. "What kind of company was this?" he thought, "what a community of theatre!" He saw that some of the actors thought a lot of themselves, decided they were pretty handsome and he suspected that the director was partial to having attractive young men around. They played their scene and made up 'business' that actors like to do and were pleased with their progress.

Eventually the time came for Harry's little speech, somewhat delayed by the amount of time the director had given to the actor who had been so wooden. Despite all the coaxing, the notes and advice had only served to make the actor worse as he suffered under the exposure of the director's fraying attention. Satisfaction for Harry. He would show the director how a worthy actor had been overlooked, how he would have done a much better job and the director would rue his decision and regard him with a new eye. The play at last came to his scene and, instead of waiting for direction, he just did it straight through. It was unexpected and left a silence in its wake. It was done better than the part demanded and he was a better actor than he should have been. It was defined, sharp, stylish and, not only had it been unexpected, it was also unnecessary. The director, however, seemed pleased with it and let it pass on. The day ended with a tiny upbeat, but eventually that pleasant sensation diminished as the long, early, summer evening stretched out fretfully. Harry went to his digs, wrote letters and read and gnawed on the choking gag of his loneliness... but the weekend would surely arrive and, after the Saturday morning rehearsal, Harry would flee from his bier of loneliness, from the dark, soulless city that crushed all humanity out of people.

That week was the longest week of his life with endless boring hours of repetition that the director hoped would change the sour milk of the play into butter, but it was getting nowhere, the director seeming to acknowledge the fact with his increasingly angry outbursts. Now that the director had 'blocked' the play and run through the scenes, he allowed a simpering, effete drip, who was employed as a trainee director or assistant, to take some of the rehearsals of the group scenes while his boss concentrated on the leading roles. The toady sat oozing himself into the stalls and provided, no doubt, some much needed genital relief to the director. He had one of those faces that looked as if it had been born with a sneer; a rubber fleshy face in which two furtive eyes were placed like grapes in a bowl of custard. When it came to Harry's scenes, which he now performed with a certain élan and which even drew a measure of respect from the other actors, the slimy assistant, on giving notes, passed a comment that it looked 'awkward and amateurish!' Harry knew in his urine that the jerk was lying and, whatever reason compels the spit of venom to rise in men's mouths, one didn't have to look far in the case of this sullen wretch. Harry irked the assistant by being accomplished in his role. There was nothing for rubber face to say, no notes to give and the assistant director's role was made slightly defunct. He preferred actors whose 'needs' made him feel all powerful and wise. Harry did not give him that. The assistant went on in his slippery way that he meant Harry to take "awkward and amateurish" as a compliment since he felt that the character should be clumsy and inept as he struggles in a small, village fair for attention. Harry had never heard such rubbish in his life but knew where it came from since the turd could not simply say "Well done." He had to condemn his acting in order to make himself feel superior, but then add that it was adequate, nay, even most suitable, for the role. And this said in front of everyone.

"Pisspot!" Harry thought. "Good, keep it like that," the director's arse-licker lisped. Harry drained epithets from hate-filled areas of his brain like he was drawing phlegm and wished to spit them at him, but just looked at him as if his whole existence was of no consequence. The director had liked it and that was all that mattered. The assistant was merely a fat, white worm that Harry would like to step on. But Harry did add that he "didn't realise that it came across like that." He still somehow couldn't believe what he was hearing and hoped the assistant might even rephrase it, but he only went on to repeat his opinion with even more emphasis when he saw he'd drawn Harry's blood. The scum had far less knowledge of the theatre than Harry, even if he was playing a smaller part than his experience warranted. The assistant was intoxicated with his temporary power over the actors and was using it clumsily. Harry restrained himself, which was all he could do, and his own vulnerability allowed his malicious spittle to leak its way back into his own soul, creating a nasty taste of doubt.

Saturday did eventually come, rewarding him with some celebratory sunshine and he found a bus that took him most of the way to his lady's home in the countryside. After a long journey he got there in time for tea. He entered the house and walked straight into the garden without saying more than a word. It was late afternoon and she was fondly expecting him. The heavy branches of the trees swayed caressingly in the breeze and a teapot was soon to arrive on the wooden, garden table accompanied by toasted, brown bread. Harry couldn't speak. He sat and could not believe this blissful, beautiful happiness where love flowed with no restraint. He just sat there and let the acid that had accrued that week pour out of his eyes. He cried with joy, with relief, with satisfaction ... with *sheer* relief ...

The following weeks of rehearsal would never be as bad again. The production was a respectable flop and the actors in the company, and whose careers Harry would read about from time to time in a *The Stage*, gradually faded away into a sea of obscurity. Except the star who did go on to fulfil the early promise of his youth, and of course... Harry.

BIG FISH

Big Fish

It was a big one! Oh yes, it was one of those whoppers that you catch once in a while, sometimes once in a lifetime and, like Hemingway's *The Old Man and the Sea*, once you have your hook into it, you can't let go. You grab the part eventually with hungry, raw, bleeding hands while it thrashes and twists out of your grasp, throwing you all over the place as it seeks to escape back into the pages, not letting you chew it up until it becomes part of your bloodstream, part of your reflexes. A new role becomes a friend who moves in with you and for whom you have to adjust, get to know, understand, not battle with too often and not give in to – but establish a modus vivendi with. But it is also a thing that moves inside you like a demon that you must exorcise each night lest it grow mad with incarceration. When you have mastered it you will feel only a benevolent incubus that no longer revolts or causes you to sweat with fear, but allows you the joy of riding it, for you have learned how to touch the beast.

Or else, seeking yet another metaphor for this so elusive thing, this fusing of flesh and word, it is a shadow reverberating against the million memories in your own mental archive. The shadow draws from your life to give it colour, warmth and humanity, and in this way it also resembles a vampire that sucks your soul while you sleep. The role is also a homeless beggar rummaging around your dustbin until it or he finds what is serviceable and useful for his needs. You are the great dung heap of experience that the character plunges into, and even if you think you are creating the character as you rummage in the wigs and props department, it is growing almost by itself. Sometimes too much conscious interference will spoil it and so as you sleep, it slowly feeds on your mind until you change, subtly, slowly into the being that the author has designed for you, for the author is the real brain who conceived the character out of the million memories in his own library. Your blood merely feeds it even if, when you take the curtain call, you will not be able to separate, no, not for a second, what royalty the author has of the applause, and what share is yours. You will have confused the two and become Frankenstein's monster, thinking you created yourself when in fact your body, with its amazing variety of sensations, is the food for the host. The author's words play your memory and life until they find the right tune, a little of this and a dash of that until you and the part harmonise.

Then you play the wonderful symphony of words, or do the words play the wonderful symphony of you? You think otherwise, since that is the way you greedily suck in the oxygen of the applause, revelling in it as if you had not only played the part but had written it, fleshed it, and given it life. But the reverse is nearer the truth, that you the actor were a dead thing, without much purpose beyond satisfying the basest and crudest desires and that the author gave you a life you never dreamed of and turned a simple player into a brilliant philosopher, poet, and duellist. You bow with the sweat dripping down your face as if it were blood trickling down from your crown of thorns. You believe you are like a wine taster, approving, analysing and making the right judgement, but here the analogy ends, since the wine is really tasting you and then spitting you out after making its judgement.

Or is it memories that shape who we are and what we do? From moment to moment like little children, (since our most powerful memories may stem from childhood) we scurry around feverishly searching for a game so that we can come out and play. That's why we call it a play, so that we can escape from the meaningless ritual of our lives, play with our 'memories' and let them live all over again. But is it the actor interpreting the writer, or the writer interpreting the actor, allowing the actor to understand himself? Who he is. This is who I am. I am this. This is really me. I am like this person. These are my feelings. I am sensitive like the hero. Yes, I am a sentient being. I am a brave person. Romantic. Passionate. Loving. But can be a funny, wild rascal. All those things. They are me. Really. Yes. I am just a cocktail of emotions. I am Herod. Harlequin. The golem. Hamlet. I am a man in search of a soul. I am anima and animus.

So the charge of words set off a chain reaction in Harry as he carefully read the part he was to audition for, since what he read in the role was HIMSELF! Never had he read anything that so carefully probed what he felt, those formless, inchoate sensations, that peculiar sense of FAILURE that seemed to track him like a ghost. Yes, here it was in this play, but made heroic, majestic, movingly beautiful. The WORDS gave shape to what in him was vile, needy, desperate and insecure and yet made those negative qualities significant, touching and poetically romantic. An audience would weep for a person like this, who in the street would

47

be an object of utter contempt to them, but lift him into the spotlight as a sacrifice, separated by a stage-like moat like some wild beast in a zoo, and he would be seen as an object of fascination and pity. This character had to be Harry. The author must have had similar fears, feelings of inferiority, lack of self-worth, creating from these an anti-hero, whose moods echo what Harry had so often felt. Now he had found a friend in this character and swiftly learned the speeches, which quickly adhered to his mind having found a safe, warm home in which to incubate. Harry was the perfect host!

Yes, the play wakened Harry's old doubts, but this in turn fed the character; the speeches were infused with all the horrible desperation that lay like a silent lake deep within him, and now it was all allowed to come gushing out in a thick spouting geyser. The writer's words loosened up the debris in the old dilapidated house that was Harry. The collapsed masonry was now being restored, as the voice grew stronger and the emotions raced along the circuitry of his brain, fired the boilers, and a rumbling was heard in Harry's mind and lights were flashing on. Now the bolts were pulled back in their rusty sockets, doors were creaking open and windows raised for the air to come rushing in, and the mould withered and fresh wind ventilated the house. Harry was feeling himself again. The words gently moved the tumblers that opened the safe and inside was his musty, old soul. The words sang around his mind, the right buttons were pressed, the penny dropped, the bell rang and the ALARMS WENT OFF! Yes, he had fused with the play and when he went to read for it, he already knew that the play was written for him. It might have been. He might have been a model for the author. It was a play about a youngish man, past his prime, who cannot connect to the world and its values and therefore feels himself to be an outsider. He becomes a lonely, desperate being and seeks communication with a stranger whom he meets in a neutral environment, a park. He needs to tell the stranger, who represents 'normal' society, what life is like for a person who, for whatever reason, has never managed to enter the door to that society. He forces the stranger to listen to him so that his story, however pathetic and horrible, may stir the stranger to make some kind of gesture of acknowledgement to him, as if he were a supplicant showing his wounds and seeking alms.

So yes, drama makes no distinction between the 'haves' and the 'have nots,' since both are grist to its mill, and Harry is grateful that the effluvium of human society seeks its outlet through the pores of the drama. It is the less noble aspects of the human soul that the playwright finds so fascinating. While Harry may find that society protects itself against his desperate needs, girding its loins against the beggar; the writer, like a scientist, examines the strange abominations of the human soul. He extracts the pain and the horror and uses it as flavouring for his verbal stew. Drama casts its spotlight on the warped, the different, the odd, the pained, the very poor, the suicidal, and the outsider, and paradoxically the 'hero,' since this is what we deign to call the deformed protagonist who in every aspect seems to fit Harry. Like a second skin. Not simple but curved, twisted, bizarre and curious. Harry slipped his body into the creature and, yes, it fits like it was made to measure, and needs minimal adjustment. Like the great theatrical non-conformist and madman, Antonin Artaud, who felt that only he could play the hypersensitive and diseased character portrayed in Edgar Allan Poe's *The Fall of the House of Usher* since he *was* Roderick Usher, so Harry, too, found his alter ego. Yes he found himself described, for he too clawed at the door and scratched at the window begging to be let in. Yet he is only allowed to be witnessed at a safe distance like a beast on a stage, so that we may feel pity and terror, and relief that we can go into the street, and escape from the loathsome pit of screeching humanity and lock our doors.

So Harry had found a partner in crime and embraced him. Words roared around his mind and Harry became the character and the character fed on Harry. Like a filthy duo they wrapped themselves round each other, coiled snakes mating on a tree. When he read at the audition for the director, the man was surprised and a little disturbed by the ease with which Harry slipped inside the role. Of course he was given the part, since the actor whom the director had earmarked for the role was not free to do it. No, he was on a film that would never end. The great Orson Welles was directing, and so Harry, by one stage removed, was grateful to Orson. Thank you, Mr. Welles!

However that may be, he was more suited and bled into the soul of the character far more than the mere actor they had wanted for it. Harry had brewed his blood until it had become bile; bile ran through his veins and he fed the incubus with it, gently nurturing the beast, the killer, the avenger. The audience would watch and be horrified and laugh at the horror and disgusting manifestation of the character's actions, his pathetic needs, his abject and crude desires, his isolation from the warm pleasures of

CIVILISATION. They would watch and feel pity, and at the end would shed a little tear for the poor man who was so funny and witty and sad.

On the day of the reading Harry took the Tube to the end of the line, where the theatre remained after everything else in the area had been knocked down, like a cultural lighthouse standing in a sea of grey urban conformism. The director knew he had a live one in Harry, and knew also that in some way Harry had ingested the role and it was growing inside him like a child of Satan. Each day he got the Tube to the remote theatre and each day the thing grew and grew until he felt he had to restrain it, hold it back for he was becoming the person and the person was sucking on Harry's soul. And yet he knew that he must not allow his new friend to take over, for there must be enough of him left to peep above the surface and allow him to navigate. Eventually the first night came and the nerves were building up almost to snapping as the creature sought to be born. The other actors with whom, as expected, he had hardly any relationship (the character he played seemed to act as a deterrent to any chumminess) were busy opening their telegrams, sinking their bouquets of well-wishers' flowers into vases, giving each other little trinkets and winks, 'good lucks,' 'break legs', crossed fingers, adjusting their make-up. Few cards came for Harry, sitting alone in his dressing room.

Now Harry was in the first act only, meant as a kind of curtain-raiser to the main event, but that's not how he saw it. He was about to make the first act the main event and he sat, looked in the mirror and waited. He smoked a cigarette and went over the first few lines.

"Beginners please!" ... Harry was half-asleep, drugged with fear and nervous energy that can sometimes put you into a semi-conscious state. His fellow actor, with whom he shared the first act, nodded a good luck, as Harry did to him. In those days, there were no nice little previews to help you get your nerves together; in those days you opened and the critics saw you the first time that you exposed your performance to the eyes and ears of the audience. Harry walked on stage and waited. The curtain was still down and he heard the audience, a great hungry stomach rumbling in the distance. He breathed slowly. The curtain rose... a giant eyelid and revealed Harry just standing there. He had the first lines and he started speaking to the stranger. When the evening ended the whole world knew who Harry was.

YMCA

YMCA

Harry didn't mind the trip to Victoria too much. It got him out of the house and he could always bump into a mate or two on the dole queue who would later join him at a café for an hour of actorly gossip. He found the usual group of people who were just as animated as he was to see each other. Each had left a room or flat where unemployment hung around their heads like ether and rendered them sluggish and indifferent to the outside world. At such times the sanctuary of the home turned into a prison that they had no good reason to leave. Signing on at least forced one to leave the house, get on the Tube and start motions that might lead to other useful activities. In Harry's case, he would pop into the YMCA at Tottenham Court Road which in those days had an excellent, albeit run down gym for men only where you could sweat some of the aggro out of your being. This was the old, original YMCA before they rebuilt it and let in *women*!

Nothing really wrong with that, but a lot of the men were pissed off because they were made to wear vests. Before then you'd play handball without one, or until it became soaked through and then you'd discard it. But now you had to play with this wet thing on; and there were other complaints... Females inhibiting our camaraderie, and loud yacking. On the benefit side, it made everybody clean up their act and stop wearing that smelly, torn gym-wear, worn affectionately until it nearly fell off. But those were the old YM days.

He made an exit from the tube opposite Lyons Corner House, crossed the road, entered the large Victorian building, walked downstairs to the gym, got his basket out in which his old sweat shirt, shorts and plimsolls were kept (a most unhygienic practice, later abandoned), found a locker, changed and then meandered onto the handball court. Two couples were using both courts, battering away furiously, and so he hung around waiting for one of them to be free but meanwhile challenged the winner, since you weren't allowed more than two games when others were waiting. Once you were on that court it was hard to leave, so liberating was it to play; and what a relief when you were unemployed to be able to use your body, wit, strength, timing, and sweat all the poisons out. Sheer relief. And the sweetness of the shower afterwards, washing all away until you came out clean, raw and light.

So Harry said... "Play the winner?" which was half a question and half a demand and, since everybody had to abide by the rules, nobody really minded, except the cab drivers who had been there for as long as Harry could remember and always commandeered the court. Somehow the fury of the game, played almost daily, kept them forever young and all you needed was a tennis ball, a wall and some strong hands. So in other words, it's a real working-class game.

Harry wasn't a bad player, which he wryly put down to the amount of unemployment he had to endure but, on the other hand, even a working actor will seldom do more than nine months a year, and so there was always time to go to the YM. An old man had taught him, more as an act of need than charity, since few would play with the old fella anymore. He liked training newcomers so that he would have a partner until that partner demanded tougher opponents. Once in the gym, even old guys became kids again and fooled and joshed around, told you off, mocked your serve, hooted when their return smashed the ball where you didn't expect it. But you learned, and Harry could still remember the old guy with the bald head who would throw the ball a little in the air, let it bounce once and then hit it. Harry had developed his serve and could use either hand, and by balling his hand into a fist, then smashing the ball, it bounced off the wall with greater speed than an open-handed serve. He badly needed a game, needed to sweat, to be involved, to move, prance, crouch, return a difficult ball, slide across the floor, kill the ball by aiming low. Yes, he could be quite an opponent and that redeemed him for a while. However, no matter how much he played and tried to improve his game, there were one or two players who seemed unbeatable and played with awesome skill. Of course they played every day of their lives. Two of these 'super-players' he knew worked in the printing trade off Fleet Street and Covent Garden. He noticed that the better the player, the more modest the person, as if there were some relationship between the two.

There was a particular pair who used to play each other most days as if they were betrothed on the handball court. One of them wore the thick, pebble-lensed glasses, so beloved of working-class people, and had one of those pure Anglo-Saxon faces; beaky nose, clear white skin, like an Arthurian knight in brass-rubbings. He had such a pleasant demeanour, one could take him for a Buddhist. The game was his form of meditation since he played it with real devotion. Sometimes Harry wouldn't go to the YM for months, on the rare occasion a tour took him away from London, but on returning to the YM he would see these two playing and Harry was reassured by their presence. They were a sign that life, the gym and handball were forever, since the pair never seemed to get any older. One of them would always knock up a few balls for a warm-up with Harry, while waiting for his partner to arrive, and on these occasions he felt privileged to play with one of the masters. Yet, no matter how many hours he put into the game, and no matter how many years, there was a intangible barrier that prevented Harry getting any better. Harry could play hard and beat good players, but with these two dedicated players he found it difficult to score even one point. They possessed a kind of magic.

The taxi drivers used to hog the courts, but he guessed they needed it after being cramped up in their cabs for hours at a time. They played game after game, laughing, sweating, joking and commenting on each other and were highly fit from their daily work-outs. When Harry wanted a game there was always someone else 'waiting,' and so he would often wait around for a partner, only to find at the end that everyone had gone and all he could do was get dressed again, with the bile still lodged in his bloodstream that he had been unable to purge by a good smash against a wall.

Yes, he was good, since he was here for long stretches of time when unemployment drove him here out of sheer need, a need as great if not greater than the taxi drivers. Then one day Harry would disappear for a few months and everyone knew he had been working and when he returned they would all chime, "Where've you been?" Although the absence meant he lost a bit of edge, he was still a formidable opponent, good enough to beat most except the printers. But he could beat almost all of the second division players, (in which he counted himself). On one inspired occasion, playing at full strength, he scored 21-0 against an Indian gentleman whom he often played and with whom he usually had well-matched games. The Indian was always as pleased to see Harry as Harry was to see him, and they settled down to two or three games with much smiling and "well done" and "shot!" when either retrieved a difficult serve or volley. It was a relationship that lasted years although they never saw each other outside the gym. Within the gym they might have been brothers. The 21-0 was an anomaly and it was never mentioned in the future years. It was as if it had never happened.

When Harry was 'accepted' for a game with a first division player who was already steaming and sweating from his triumphs, he would still be allowed a few minutes grace for a warm-up when they would knock the ball against the wall. It was sportsmanship, if you'd been playing for a while, to give your opponent time to warm up the palms and get the hips swivelling. To determine who serves first, both players throw the ball against the wall and whoever gets nearest to a thin strip of wood that marks the end of the wall is the server. Harry threw the ball and was closest. He dropped the ball, let it bounce once and then smashed it as hard as he could with his gloved fist, unusual since a fist has less control than a hand, but it whacked the wall hard and shot off at that extra speed which sometimes made returns difficult. Often the opponent would be grateful just to get this killer serve back, but then Harry would kill the ball by slamming it low. So the game continued and he warmed up. The first welcome trickles of sweat ran down his flushed face, the angst slowly slipping out of his body. Whelps of joy came out as he served his torrential blows and the ball sprang back from the wall like a missile. Yes, he was in his glory. His body was ALIVE.

The other player soon got used to the serve and then it was his opponent's turn. Harry was outfoxed and leaped for the small, darting shadow and crashed sometimes to the floor to return it, clambered up, served again, smashed, feinted, dropped it suddenly close to the wall. The opponent would race to save it, colliding with the wall as he did, softening the impact with his hands, and the impact of his dash would make him try to kill the ball. Harry, anticipating this, would already be speeding back. But the opponent would also guess that this was exactly what Harry would do, and so would pat the ball gently as if he were tickling a cat under the chin. And now Harry would fly back, miss, and shout with exaggerated frustration like he had just been whipped. A long yell. How good it was to let your feelings out and so nakedly express them: the yelps of praise, gasps of shock, shouts of triumph, groans of disappointment, murmurs of irony, chortles of mockery, moans of disbelief... all sounds and no words. A second game ensued. Whack, smash, dip, sway, curve, crunch, spin, and the bodies were leaving their sweat on the wooden floor and along with the sweat the acid, the angst, the rot, the decay, the waiting, the listlessness, the staleness, the agony, the hurt, the anger, and as it was being sluiced out in a pool of sweat the face and the body were shining, gleaming and pink.

They finished their two games and democratically won one game each and at the end the players took off a glove and touched hands. Oh the relief, the blessed, wonderful, exhilarating, freeing, liberating ecstasy of it all. In the showers the liquid felt like silk and the shampoo ran into his eyes, and they joked and jostled, giggled and yacked; their voices rising ever higher to overcome the water pounding their bodies. Harry washed away the dirt and the frustration, washed it all away in the rancid, smelly old gym. The showers were old and musty and the soap he bought at the desk was a thin, white slab, cheap and institutional smelling, but it was washing it all away. The two men had made a *pas de deux*, sprung, like animals chasing a prey, challenged each other's skill, energy, force and heart and yes, it was good!

Yes, he was indeed alive again, using himself and being used, alert, sharp reflexes being put to service. The waterfall of water rid him also of the sins, the crimes against his nature, the overeating, the smoking, the drinking, the abusing of his male, abundant, human, energy that he couldn't always use for his art and which became sour. His strength, his life became a dead thing rotting under a floorboard, stank inside his spirit. But now he burned, he melted, he felt used and the rain of warm abundant water baptised him pure.

He left the shower and dried, still in the same spirit of joy, vigorously pulling the crisp, white towel across his shoulders... forwards and backwards, rubbed it up and down his thighs, stuck a morsel in his ear, checked himself in the mirror, put his sweaty clothes back in the basket to dry out until reused, and collected his membership card. He felt on top of the world as he descended the steps of the old YMCA, enjoyed the cool wind caressing his cheeks and walked to the Tube. As he sat there, he sensed the first stirrings of sadness creep. He had nothing to express with this fit, alive, reborn body.

He got out at Finsbury Park, walked down Woodberry Grove to his flat and when he got in, made himself a cup of tea and pondered what he must do next. Having reached no conclusion, and now feeling a little guilty that this revitalised body had no further challenges, he decided to coarsen it a bit and lit a cigarette.

FILTHY BASTARD
DIRECTORS!

Filthy Bastard Directors!

Filthy, (fucking) white, Nazi trash! Yes, that's what he thought, somewhere deep within his craw where, with the devotion of a miser hoarding his gold, Harry had stored his rejections until the fierce juices of his hatred had turned them into an acid bath. Here he mentally dipped his victims as they sat there in the stalls and coldly thanked him for his pains in tones of supercilious superiority. What did they know, slovenly bastards from Oxford who ponced all their lives off the state? Kept at university, vaguely studying some literature that someone else had to guide them to, and were eventually employed by the slum rotting minds who had trodden the same iniquitous path. What did they know of struggle, of working on a building site, standing in a dole queue, serving in a dirty, grotty pub, waiting tables in a smart restaurant where you'd hide your head in shame when an actor or director of your acquaintance came to dine? Then you felt doubly shamed; one, for the humiliating work that you were being forced to do and, two, for not having the guts to accept it and boldly march out and greet them. What did they know of suffering, anguish or the reverberations inside the human soul that was downstairs washing glasses since Harry preferred the anonymity of the kitchen basement doing chores than upstairs, where his shame was wrapped round him with an apron.

Art was for them received and learned but never lived. It was literature, texts, classics, metre, and humans were just the toys of blood used by these traders of flesh, for that's what they were; pimps, dealers in the long line of bodies at a slave auction lined up to serve, playthings that they could move around like toy soldiers. They couldn't even speak to you... they had no words... nothing to say... had no sentences, no sounds, no common ground of recognition, no humanity, or spirit, for they never lived in life as did the actor in his nightly grind; when given the opportunity to work that is, the actor matched his nerves to the audience. What did they really know of an actor's craft, of the workings of his voice, heart, muscle, skeleton, language, breath, harmony and dreams? They couldn't know actors, knew not what to do with them except place them against pretty, decorative sets, and push them around after having first worked out the moves at home with their little, toy soldiers in their little, model sets. Knew not the smell of slum flats, piss stinking, broken-down lifts, overcrowded kitchens, alienated mums and dads. Tube trains at 7am, standing for years in dreary shops whilst they were lying in the grass reading Milton and worrying what iambic pentameters were so that they could bamboozle their slaves with phoney science since they had no other method of communication which might have in it love, friendship, comradeship ... nothing. Two line letters of rejection from directors for whom you gave your life blood and even bailed out. A broken sentence or two. "Yes – er – thank you, but I've planned ahead for the season and – er..."

Dead white flaccid flesh, knew no joyous games as children when you played forever in the street as if the day would have no end and there was no end to the games that were continually invented so that you might retain the loving sweetness of your best friend for a few minutes more. You hugged your friends, grabbed them by the shoulders, caught them in a neck-lock, wrestled them to the floor, leapfrogged over their backs, climbed with them over fences, played cricket, kicked a ball against a wall, played, always played, understood the message that passed between you, the need to play and celebrate each other's existence by means of tests, rituals, daring, leaping from high walls, and who could jump from higher? Even fighting, yes, even sometimes in the heat of passion, in the confusion of needs, to risk the bony encounter but that was rarely, very rarely with friends. But all these myriad ways told you and your dear friend exactly who you were and what you meant to each other... Then you grew up... worked... received pay packets and one day you decided to try acting and so it became necessary to desert your mates. You left them to do other things, and so became an actor, the messenger of the gods, for still you wished to play, to celebrate, to create, to give, to make patterns, to challenge, to test your prowess, to grapple with language, the scorching fires of exposure, the testing in the raw, live world of the audience.

But the yellow-faced, simpering turd just down from uni was taking the auditions; the loathsome, round, spotted, ugly, flaccid face who never got to grips with anything more than his dick, who devotedly licked his master's arse and stank of bullshit, the whoremaster, this pug. Hotspur from *Henry IV* springs to mind who describes an amateur who has authority merely because he has a whiff of culture and a drop of blue blood...

"*Came there a certain lord, all neat and trimly dressed, fresh as a bridegroom, and his chin new reaped showed like a stubble land at harvest time...*"

So did this face of whey, like a plate of unspeakable porridge sitting on his scrawny neck in the stalls, constipated with theory, drunk with self-importance, bloated with stupidity and sterile from lack of fertilisation in real, human society. And yet Harry, while certainly no enemy of art, knowledge or intellect, despised these permanent sponges for the ease with which they slithered through life, linking up and fusing with like-minded, spineless, theatrical groupies and literary morons who had not the faintest idea of what constitutes an actor. Yes, they might know how to analyse a line but would never know how to bring it to life, to express the heart of it or move it, say it, relate it. In other words, they had not the art of the game; actors being for them merely creatures that they manipulated but did not play with, could not, and never did. Never.

No, they watched. On stage, after an actor spoke his lines he was dead, still, limp, a human with the battery taken out. The director knew not what to do with actors who spoke not, and they truly resembled those toy soldiers, kept in a cupboard, which he had moved around the night before. So 'God' decided to fade them out of existence by draining the light from the mute players, leaving them in the dark while keeping the leading actor in the spotlight. We could be fantasy figures moving in a swirling mist of dry ice, or be left standing still on a revolving stage, lowered on pulleys, raised on lifts, or any other of the multitude of toys they could put their tin soldiers on; but they knew not how to move them since they knew no games. They knew the meaning of the words, but never the meaning within the human soul or the secrets of the body. Great sets were created and brilliant designers got together to help the director make up for his lack of soul, for that space in his chest.

These thoughts tumbled over and over in Harry's head as the yellow, sleek, Oxford grad stares up with his limpid expression, his subsidised, untrained body that knew no craft of the gesture or sign and could not give it or even suggest it. Can you imagine a boxing trainer who had never boxed, or a dance choreographer who had never danced? The fight trainer knew about rhythm, pace, being centred, when to strike, how to feint, duck, deliver the big one. At least how to breathe even... train... to be fit... alive. All these bandits knew was how to con, fool, deceive with words, confuse with artifice and "When I speak let no dog bark." So the round-faced monkey in the stalls had dismissed him. To relieve himself of the pain, Harry had summoned up all the demons he could so he could dip into his little acid bath, these inept jerks who had to call in a movement adviser for the least little piece of action. They could do nothing except resemble themselves, make pictures that came close to the flaccid one they saw in the mirror. The ghastly image of themselves they saw in the mirror. The foul toad that stared back at them as they gazed in awe at themselves in the mirror. The round, soggy face from the stalls expected Harry to go off-stage after this brief dismissal, expected him to be absorbed back into the anonymous space from whence he had materialised like a cloud of atoms forming out of the air, like a golem created from clay.

Harry had come and with goodwill had laid his audition on the stage but now was expected to dematerialise and sink back into the darkness. He was expected to go. The director's eyes longed for an empty space... for the stage to be free of the thing that made him feel uneasy, and like all the others before him, the actor should go so that the director could stare at nothing for a while until the next lump of flesh materialised. Harry hadn't worked for six months and was already tight for time to get back across London to his part-time job in the pub. The shift began at 5pm but he lingered as if to remember the blob of phlegm in front of him, or to relish just a few seconds more of being on that stage, or a bit of both. Harry stood, sweat trickling down his forehead from the recent effort, and sensed that he had no luck; but that was normal, that he was used to, that he could cope with, since his style was different and could not easily be accommodated by those who were set in ways of their own. Even so, let there be a small, red tongue of goodwill that like a magic carpet he could exit on.

The sallow, simpering shit simply had no understanding of pain. The animal's pain that you, vile, wretched parasite in the stalls will use to validate your life, to make you feel clever, worthwhile, innovative, bright. "Oh! What an original way of seeing it, darling, and your *Cherry Orchard* was wonderful." We are the blood and viscera you shunt about so you can play with us. Play with your toys of warm souls. Harry turned on his heel satisfied that somehow his message had etched itself on the brain of the assistant director who was standing in for his master. Harry marched down the street wishing he had someone to play with.

RESTING

Resting

Tired, he was always tired lately... not during the day when the city's population flowed through the streets, as if a tide had been let loose on parched fields, and carried Harry like a piece of flotsam on the back of its surging force. The river of flesh flowed into nooks and crannies – holes, stairs, doors, lifts, cafés, museums – a human lava flow that would not be stopped until it had reached its destination, paused for the time it needed to accomplish its goals and then, like a tide, was sucked back into the suburbs from whence it came. But in the meantime Harry was deposited... a piece of debris in the heart of the metropolis. There he had a purpose, could browse around the bookshops, slip through the labyrinth of streets designated as Soho, idle in the National Gallery, sip a coffee in Patisserie Valerie – a favourite haunt in Old Compton Street, scour the antique stalls of Camden Passage, Islington's seventeenth century backstreets, visit the YMCA if in the mood, sign on at the Labour Exchange, call a chum and have a breakfast chinwag in the local greasy spoon or nag the agent. There were a thousand and one other things an unemployed actor in London could do to kill the time, swept along on the stream of human activities, and at any of these places there might occur a chance meeting with some eminently desirable and unattached woman.

Even, and this was always an option, visit the Astoria Dance Hall in Charing Cross Road, where each afternoon an event quaintly called tea-dancing took place. The hours were from 3pm to 6pm and, as you entered, the outside world vanished as the band played the current hits of yesteryear that housewives, widows, couples and au pair girls might find appealing. Yes, the Astoria Dance Hall was the last hope café, the refuge and sanctuary for those who did not have a large role to play in helping to keep the great metropolis going round and, for Harry, who literally did not have a role to play, it was a way of turning away from the accusing light of day and basking in ersatz night. Here he could purge his frustrated energy and translate it into pure, fevered lust in the pursuit of some desirable, interested, fascinating piece of female flesh. This not only took one's mind away from the frenzied world outside, but seemed an alternative and worthwhile pursuit for which he, for some reason, had no guilt. Yes, today he would go tea-dancing. So he took the Tube, changed at Holborn for the Central Line and exited when the train stopped at Tottenham Court Road, stared with almost unseeing eyes at the brassiere ads that moved past him on the escalator and blinked with pleasure as he entered the bustle of Oxford Street.

After the claustrophobia of the Tube the sudden shock of the city never failed to surprise him, and he took his familiar walk around the corner to Charing Cross Road and descended the stairs into the warm, amber, subterranean cavern. It was also womb-like, a soft, crimson, velvety room where sperm-filled men pursued egg-filled ladies in a furious dance and maybe one or more lucky spermatozoa would eventually penetrate. As he trod the thickly-carpeted stairs he felt he was sinking slowly into a bath of warmth and music which gradually enveloped, covered and swallowed him up, filling his ears, his nose and then his eyes. First he took in the syrupy music and then the blur of moving bodies sweeping around the floor, and finally his nose detected their combined scents sweetening the atmosphere with its sensual mix. Couples were swirling around the floor in a waltz, tightly held females of all shapes and sizes, making their ritualistic perambulation, moving anticlockwise but why this was always the fashion one never knew. He grimly observed that they seemed to be mostly an older lot today, middle-aged ladies from North London swathed in taffeta or flowing floral dresses, hair frozen into a wave of candy floss and just as stiff, as he had noticed on one occasion when desperation made him charter one of them for a short but choppy voyage round the floor. The experience, combined with the penetrating odour of her hair lacquer, made him positively seasick.

Apart from Harry, who had arrived rather early, there was the usual gaggle of hirsute men in suits, pushing their live baggage around like porters at King's Cross Station. They were mostly waiters and kitchen staff from Soho who had just come off the lunch shift and had a couple of hours to kill. Some went to the betting shop, others idled their afternoon chatting in a coffee bar in Greek Street, a few went home, and some ended up at the Astoria to see what they could fondle and squeeze for their two or three hours of freedom before once more grovelling in front of the tables of Kettners, L'Escargot, or the Gay Hussar. Waiters and chefs were notorious womanisers, since this was for them a chance to get a grip on what they had to dance around and cater for at the table, a kind of revenge. Some were remarkably seedy, he noticed, as a swirling, moustachioed dancer had protruding from his tight and ill-fitting jacket, a folded copy of *The Evening Standard* open at the racing page.

Harry sat and calmly surveyed the room, waiting for it to fill up a little and then would turn into a predatory animal ready to pounce on a single female sitting alone. He quite liked the young ones, particularly French au pair girls. Loneliness and desperation for some human contact had driven them to ride this carousel of the flesh. The dance ended and a couple who seemed entwined as if joined at the hip like Siamese twins, parted suddenly, each exploding off in different directions with no music to glue them together any more, or justify embracing a complete stranger. Each wandered off into the gloom from whence they had emerged, and then the band-leader, looking bored under his grinning mask, made an effort to bare his teeth and announce that the next dance will be Latin American, in fact a samba. There was about as much resemblance to Latin America in this faded English dance-hall as a holiday poster – just an image – a shadow, and then the group of balding, sweaty musicians smiled happily as is mandatory from those of Latin temperament and shook their tambourines. A few stalwarts got up, albeit sheepishly, since the rhythm demanded a floss more energy than was required for the grope waltz or foxtrot. Harry would sit this one out too, but nevertheless made his trajectory around the floor in the affectedly casual way men have of pretending that they are just taking a leg-stretch round the room. Here in the dance hall, the genetic signals were reaching back into the inner coils of the brain, echoing a time when the predator would be circling its prey on the open savannah in some vast Africa at the dawn of time. In the shimmering distance was a young deer grazing and Harry concealed himself in the long grass. Here there was an attractive, dark-haired, young woman standing alone, smoking a cigarette. Harry would have liked to ask her to dance and lingered somewhat, trying to be inconspicuous, turning his head this way and that, as if not in the least interested in making a pounce. Yet as he looked back at her with almost indecent longing, she allowed herself to be whisked off by a gent of Italianate appearance. She danced without too much expression but held the steps. Harry was now able to study her lithe figure which acquitted itself well in a sheath-like dress which hugged her form a little too possessively. She did move gracefully, he anguished, and was about five foot seven which he liked. She performed the side to side motions of the dance with ease, and while the Italian kept trying to draw her closer to his needy flesh, she was able to keep her pelvis at a good distance from his, Harry noted with satisfaction.

He navigated the room observing the general melée of peroxided ladies who were mostly in pairs. There were the usual devotees who loved the art of dance, and were among the few who came expressly for that reason and knew their favourite partners. These women flowed around the room with athletic abandon. Others were seen changing their shoes as soon as they entered the dance hall, removing the tatty old, battered, street shoes and donning elegant pumps with pointed heels, putting the old ones in a carrier bag. Now, like Cinderellas, they were transformed by the shoes. Shoes can do wonders for people. They can turn a dowdy housewife into a flying, spinning, whirling confetti of flesh. Yet in spite of their expertise these women danced stiffly and reminded Harry of stick insects. The female held the male by the shoulder and as she was swept along by the wave of energy she looked away, as if all this was being done to her against her will, but still managed to follow each step and every change of her partner's body. She mustn't reveal that she enjoys the seduction. There were a few Jewish-looking matrons there who loved to gossip and dance. Here they could accomplish both at the same time, but he did notice an exotic-looking Jewess of probably Middle Eastern extraction. She was in her late thirties and wore her jet-black hair in two thick braids twined into snakes and pinned to her skull. She seemed to be on her own.

Yes, things were looking up as he marked out his potential territory; the Jewess and the younger, rather sad, but healthy-looking dancer still commandeered by the Italian; the oily concoction of medleys pouring in his ears, the confluence of scents and body odours sucked into the nose, the potential female flesh waiting, or moving, drunk up by his eyes kept his sensory functions on high alert. Without consciously thinking it, he was glad that his otherwise under-employed senses were able to extract some nourishment. He was a predator in some distant, far place, watching, listening, sniffing, each sense tuned to its highest degree of reception and was automatically interpreting all the information coming in and deciding what to do with it. He was following an instinct as old as time, even in the seedy Astoria Dance Hall, Charing Cross Road, WC2. His shoulders relaxed, his stomach softened its protective tightness, his head moved side to side with the music, a little bobbing, a touch of the hips changing weight. Hey, he was relaxing, his body going with the sound of the music – the room, a roundabout of bodies, flowers and swirling dresses. A tight skirt, with a slash that allowed one leg to be forced out, swam past. The shining domes of the band nodded to the rhythm and passed little private smirks to each other and to the band-leader who was nattily dressed in a polka-dotted shirt. Meanwhile, the off-duty waiters were grimly hanging on to their prey, trying to push their pelvises closer, hoping for a response which probably wasn't forthcoming. A thin haze of cigarette smoke was beginning to spread through the room. The women sitting in threes and fours giggled energetically, released from the bondage of their possessive spouses, relishing the variety of male flesh that they could be scornful of.

Harry studied himself in one of the many mirrors that lined the walls. Yes, fine. A thin, roll-necked sweater under a jacket... very smart but casual, hair newly shampooed and flopping over his forehead, a little on the thin side but not bad. No. Just a slight angst... the quiver in the heart and the tremor in the bubble of his oh-so-fragile confidence. He must ask the dark, saturnine, healthy-looking woman with a sad face for a dance, for she is already his in the fast-forward image of his fantasy. His projection into the unseeable future might give him the confidence of a gambler who bets to win and is empowered by hope. His future is now with her and he watches intently the movement of her body, the curve of her leg so tantalisingly shaped by her dress, the sweet, strong wave of her hips sweeping in at her waist which was held by a large, elasticated belt, and her blouse, short-sleeved, gathered and puffed out at the end, revealing healthy, tawny arms. Oh how he ached for those arms, those strong legs, those clean, powerful hands unadorned by nail-polish, her pale lipstick, swept-back hair fixed by a brooch holding the thick tresses in place. He fantasised but did not wish to hover, so circled slowly around the floor, still nonchalantly jogging his head to the music while his heart was beating a different drum. Meanwhile she was dancing the samba and hardly looking at her partner. But no, now he's talking to her, she smiles, which suddenly lights up her whole face, and now she giggles as if he has said something witty or smart and thus the swine is weaving the first of his webs around her while all Harry can do is fantasise. She must like him! Her greasy dance partner! Harry stopped obeying the rhythm of the music, stopped resembling seaweed being pulled this way and that by a tide, stopped to feel the stomach tightening again, the head heating, the jaw tensing, the teeth grinding, and felt he must move away from the source of his discomfort.

He strolled round, scanning the room, but the other potential prey were dancing and there was nothing else there he wanted, he desired, he fantasised about as much as she. He liked her strong-limbed body, so buoyant and confident of itself, and that was his match. She was his style, quality and form. He felt that he was in the same league as her. The waiter was not and never would be, and can't even be thought possible of being so. Yet damnably he *was* holding her and dancing with her. Harry turned away again and, trying to appear relaxed, noticed a brunette wallflower, rather Irish-looking, glance at him and then quickly avert her gaze, as if to pass him a signal saying, "I would not be reluctant to dance with you." He glanced once more and decided that she looked a trifle dowdy, although she had a pleasant face and certainly caused no crisis of confidence like the other, but if he danced with her he would be confirming that he was in *her* league and hence would be forever damned to remain in that division, since it was his dearest wish TO CRAWL OUT OF THAT PLACE FOREVER! No, he must ask the beauty to dance, even at the cost to his nerve. He passed the by Irish and gave her a warmish glance, rewarding her with some false sense of hope, keeping an ember glowing for an emergency. Again he swivelled his eye momentarily towards the dancer and then raked the dance floor, allowing the blurred figures to momentarily distract him from his obsession. Yes, he felt better now and was optimistic, and would be patient and wait.

Harry was a result of a million years of evolution. He must now pass on his genetic material and, whether or not *he* was aware of these things, his billion cells certainly *were.* They felt a distinct pull and were now in an uproar. Does one instinctively know one's own genetic worth that drives you to mating with those of your own 'value' and to avoid those whose 'physical' attributes seem to overwhelm yours? Harry could see that she didn't much care for the man and probably his hands were sweaty, (horrible thought) nails none too elegant, and didn't like the way he would sometimes try to push her thigh with his. Dancing can be so intimate. Yes, what a strange ritual that gives you permission to put your arm around a complete stranger and feel their body, hold their hand in yours, smell their odour, brush their thighs and then leave, like it's a test for both of you. A sniffing out in a wide-open prairie under a hot sun when two animals slowly circle each other, sniffing, examining, sensing by the highly-tuned mechanism whether the smell is strong, good, and suggests virility and health, for it has to be of equal value. Is Harry, for a second, questioning his own value and therefore his hesitancy in some basic, deep acknowledgement of his worth, and does that mean that his genetic bank cannot afford her? No. His hesitation is merely that, being so right for him, she becomes a challenge that he must face. He must not run off with the weakest doe in the herd. Do you know what happens then? Self-disgust. The dance stopped and the figures were absorbed back into the territory from whence they came as if they had marked it out; the chair, that particular patch of wall, this table. Now, ah yes, a slow waltz... good time to talk, easy to move together over the landscape as though we were taking a journey, the end of which would find us reborn as a couple.

Harry would be able to give good chat, be sensitive to her. She was adjusting her dress... the waiter had left, but no, he was HOVERING, so as to be quick off the mark for the next dance, the pig! Harry decided. Yes. Now. He walked over to her but in a way that pretended he wasn't. He strolled, so as to appear casual, but really would have liked to run across the room, snatch her hand, pull her up, and the velocity of such a gesture would throw her strong, lithe, swimmer's body into his arms, yes, feeling all that body against his; legs, thighs, her divide as his thigh moves a fraction of a second forward before hers can retreat, locking his fingers into hers, a nest of snakes, and then weightlessly whisking her off, her lips facing his, her eyes his eyes, nose to nose, smile to smile and breathing in each other's breath... yes. She would sniff him as potential genetic material. This is what Harry had somehow, in a quick flash, formed in his mind as he casually walked, and yet was he expecting rejection, or half-expecting it, and is he prepared for that half! Has he got back-up, and can he DEAL WITH THAT

FEELING WHEN YOU HAVE CROSSED THE
FLOOR, WALKED UP TO A WOMAN AND ARE
REJECTED AND FOR A MOMENT YOUR LIFE,
YOUR MOST PRECIOUS LIFE, HAS NIL MEANING?
FOR A SECOND YOU ARE IN LIMBO SINCE YOU
ARE EITHER ON THE THRESHOLD OF CREATING
A THOUSAND NEW GENERATIONS OR YOU ARE
WITHOUT PURPOSE.

But you must deal with it and the message that rejection
would imply is that your material's not suitable to mix her
chromosomes with. "Your smell is not right. My signals are
not attracted. Sorry." Yes, you deal with it, smile and walk
away, and since victims are interesting, other eyes will be
watching you, *fastened on you.* They wish to see what you
will do with the egg slowly sliding down your face! But there
is no chance of that since she danced with Mr. Greasy, and
now Harry offers her a division higher and step by step is
getting closer... She, still sitting, relaxing after the more
strenuous samba, crosses her legs, throws back her hair with
a toss of her head... she is settling. He is on his way over. His
destiny is at the end of this walk. But why? Why place so
much importance on the outcome? It's only a dance, but in
Harry's case the dance was his dance. The roles he didn't
get and the work that never expressed his ability, the hours
that sat upon his head, the hunger in the soul, the pain in
the gut, the shrivel in the balls when they are not needed for
work. You wish to use them, to challenge them, to show you
have them and here is a place where that particular rotund
receptacle is at least to be used, or could be... and so he
carries them along with his diminishing sense of self-worth,
the result of dozens of rejections. Thus like the conditioned

Pavlovian dog, poor Harry approaches the object of his hunger with the accompanying fear of receiving an electric shock, which does not make for secreting those sexual odours that women are supposed to find so attractive. So carrying both hope for the future and angst of the past, and weighed down by both, like an old Chinese water-seller with the yoke across his neck, he valiantly reaches the object of his desire. Of course, there was too much riding on this one, let alone that this should be the test before the Goddess of Fertility.

The waltz was in the first phase. Figures were darting here and there resembling fish in a tank that have just had their seed thrown in. They extricated themselves from dark corners, peeled themselves away from the wallpaper and danced into the distance. They also reminded Harry of sailing ships waiting for that sudden gust of wind to take them off into the far horizons. When the music stops the wind subsides. The ships sit quietly waiting for another gust. Harry continued to make his way as casually, slightly off-angle, as if he might make an arc past the moon, meanwhile observing the waiter, who was still hovering, poised to capitalise on his gain. Admittedly, the Italian danced quite well. Harry would now show her how *he* danced, what care *he* expressed in his motions, what sensitivity *he* possessed. This she would and must pick up from the way he handled her – his concern, poetry in motion, dry hand, warm actor's voice, strong but gentle movement. Yes, he was there! He'd arrived at the promised land, but she appeared not to have noticed this vehicle of human aspirations making his way towards her, at a slight angle of course, but she didn't even look up as he arrived at her chair. Now his voice pulled her head up to where he stood, waiting in all his glorious hope, a modest grin uncomfortably attached to his face as if it had recently been glued on.

He stood there for an eternity, the clocks stopped for a few seconds and she turned her head. It was a routine request that he had made dozens, if not hundreds of times, and sometimes they do and sometimes they don't, but on average he'd scored far more yes's, so what's the big deal? Because this one was rarer than any of the others, more exotic, what Harry had always hoped for, someone with whom he would be proud to be seen, to wait for, to look forward to seeing, to dream about, to yearn for; not like one recent pick-up, quickly steered across the street when he saw friends from his neighbourhood walking his way. So he stood there in this state. How could she possibly know the layer upon layer of crumbled hopes that formed the foundation of his request? Upon the ancient ruins of disappointment were the foundations of his new church, whatever that may be but now it was... "Care for a dance?"

She looked up, making that split-second assessment that girls have to make, and smiled. Harry moved his weight a fraction towards the ball of his foot so as to be expectantly ready, as if the request was a formality...

'No thanks,' she said, still smiling, attempting to ward off the sting of rejection with the balm of goodwill. She was tired, the previous dance had made her hot and she wanted one dance off, that's all. Perhaps there was nothing more than that which, in normal circumstances, would be the most likely interpretation; and anyway if a man can pick and choose why not grant women the same privilege? So spin on your heel, walk on, stroll past others, go to the bar, have a coffee, survey the rest, pull yourself together, and maybe even try one more time. But for reasons already well-established and that are too deep, numerous and complex, this "No thanks" was like a karate blow to shake the brain inside its fluid, causing it to knock on the walls of its cage. For him it was not just another 'no' after the thousand and one 'no's' he expected in his chosen calling; it was from *whom* the 'no' came. 'NO' – AFTER SHE HAD DANCED WITH THE GUY WHO WAS OBVIOUSLY A WAITER. THUS HER 'NO' RELEGATED HARRY TO A STATION LOWER THAN THE LOWLY AND HE SENSED THAT THE WAITER WAS WATCHING HIM AND SMIRKING WHILE STILL BEARING HER PERFUME ON HIS HAND!

Harry smiled in acceptance and turned swiftly away as if this was of no great import, but for some reason he couldn't stay in that hall, which contained the woman who would be a permanent accusation. He welcomed the cool air on his cheeks as he surfaced in Charing Cross Road. He wanted his temperature to lower but now felt sticky and hot. His hair stuck to his temples and his roll-necked sweater irritated. He didn't feel so... confident. "Fuck her," he thought, trying by demeaning his Goddess to demystify her. "How could she reject me and dance with that greasy, disgusting man... It's unforgivable. It's enough, and anyway I don't think I want to go there again ever," Harry decided. The long, metal tongue of the escalator at Tottenham Court Road gathered him up and he was transported through its dark intestines to a distant destination where the line stopped.

GRAFT

Graft

He sat in the Agent's office waiting... "Well," the agent said, "hang on," but added the rider... "if you wish"... "like the ball was in my court," Harry thought, and Shaw absolves himself from all blame. So it must be something... not fantastic, but something that Harry could make into a silk purse, since he was respected by the select few as one who could be relied on to give a small part that extra polish. Even if the agent is unaware of the intense pressure that builds up over a period of time, nevertheless he must in his position realise how even a dry crust can taste like *haute cuisine* to a starving man. What do they think we can do when unemployed? We just drop out of their minds, the way a character does in a novel whose presence is not missed until they make their entrance again and appear as familiar old friends. Harry admired the business of the agent's office, comparing it guiltily to the over-quiet emptiness of his own flat where unemployed days were like an empty canvas stretched over a frame. The secretary in the front office welcomed everyone with her usual charming efficiency and then buried herself in her work, surfacing frequently to feed the chirping phone little crumbs of consolation, never varying her carefully-worded response.

A bike messenger came into the office dressed in black shining material that stretched tightly over his bike-built muscles defining him into a piece of sculpture. His trainers looked huge, with giant flappy tongues, and cracked at the sides through effort. A mailbag was carried over one shoulder, and his peaked cap reversed to be more aerodynamic, as he streaks like a black phantom through the Soho streets. He gave the secretary a slip to sign for a package which Harry imagined the contents of, and decided by its bulk that it was probably a script for one of the agent's clients to consider. There were clients who actually had to *decide* what to accept, depending on the role's suitability, who sometimes even *turned jobs down*! Harry couldn't even begin to imagine being in a position to turn down an offer. No, he would never forget the gnawing hunger of unemployment. Yet he preferred it that way, since it confirmed his belief in the old saw that a hungry actor is a better one, and such comforting clichés gave a virtuous gloss to his unemployment.

The secretary signed the slip, and returned the clipboard back to the messenger, but let her eyes stay on his. She was bored in the office and wished to catch a glimpse of his young male energy that shone through them. Her female curiosity had been aroused by the pungent aroma of his sweat and the strong visual stimulus his body presented, and anyway it broke the boredom of office routine. He looked fit, hard, tight and busy, Harry thought, and watched enviously as the young athlete strapped in with belts, buckles and bike clips, spun on his heel and Mercury flew off into the turbulence. He reminded Harry of a black bee, buzzing from flower to flower delivering its pollen. The secretary's eyes followed his departing back, rewarding herself with a glimpse of his hard, round, small butt, then she went back to her work. However, Harry felt that she had insulted his masculinity by staring so shamelessly at the messenger, thus confirming that the other males in the room no longer presented any sexual threat; if they did, she would not have dared expose her lust with such nakedness. How attractive is vitality, he thought as he imagined the busy calf-pumping messenger bashing his testosterone through doors and, if it's only a couple of floors, flying up stairs, too impatient for things like lifts that would act as a break to his velocity, seeking the limpid eyes of receptionists, telephonists and assistants who all covet the tightly-packed meat as they let their eyes stroll slowly down his second skin.

The messenger's entrance into the office seemed to have dragged the night air in with him, since the room's temperature had definitely lowered. Harry detected the aura of cars, fumes, oil, cigarettes and streets, as if the messenger had emerged from a teeming river dragging bits of flotsam that trailed behind him. The boy's vibrant burst of energy made Harry feel idle, lazy even, decadently belonging to a pathetic profession where you spend hours sitting on seats while a comet streaks past leaving its male spore behind it. The other waiting actors all visibly shifted in their seats, as if the messenger's energy had disturbed the weeds in which they quietly contented themselves to reside. One of them, as if to shelter from the exposure the messenger's disturbance had caused, caught his eye, desperate for some mutual sympathy, and at the same time made one of those tut-tut moves that resemble a man banging a nail in with the back of his head, accompanied by a sub-vocal click of the tongue. It was a gesture of well-meaning cynicism, seeking in Harry an equally supine ally to join him in roundly condemning flaming youth and power as a life-threatening force, and if only he would make the reflecting nod back then we could link our crumbling feeble forces. But Harry instead did not wish to be identified so readily as a cohort to the aged and merely grinned back tightly and turned away leaving the man to find his own way to salvation.

The early evening deepened outside the office window. Harry thought of the crowds he would avoid now crushing themselves into canned humans by the tube-load. One of the waiting actors was in and out quickly, with a smug smile as if the news was good. A quick decision, yes or no, a season, a panto, an understudy in a safe West End run. Yes, this was an agent whose scythe didn't reap the stars, but he was good for the leftovers, and there was plenty of that for old-timers like Harry who had, by modest standards, a respectably active career of sorts; he "struts and frets his life upon the stage, and then is heard no more... a tale... full of sound and fury, signifying nothing." These little gems of Shakespeare were now embedded in the mud of his mind, and when some slight disturbance occurred they would almost involuntarily pop out. There was always some comforting thought in Shakespeare that could be made to fit almost any situation, any permutation of human experience. Harry was fond of using these pithy quotes as a verbal bandage for whatever slight wounds he suffered. He liked the fact that the player, the *actor*, was used as a metaphor by Shakespeare, since this gave Harry a sense of elevated status and helped him redeem some of the self-respect he had pawned over the years. The actor was honoured by the master, who certainly wouldn't have used a bike messenger as a metaphor for Macbeth's world weariness!

Another client had just gone in and the sitters had shuffled up a bit, quite unnecessarily he thought, since the office was now closed to any more pleas from hungry actors hoping to find a spare nipple on the agent. As they stood up and sat down again he suddenly recognised an actress from many moons ago. She gave him barely a nod of recognition but enough to say that this was all the acknowledgement she wanted, thank you very much. They didn't speak beyond that flicker between them... a light that had been accidentally switched on and then off again. As another actor provided the filling between them, they were both allowed to forget each other's existence. The receptionist, now infrequently answering the phone, found time to paint her nails with consummate skill, taking extraordinary pains to get the strokes just right. This was yet another act, he thought, that was somewhat disrespectful to the remaining clients who sat there with hopes ignited by Mr. Shaw's request for them to, "Hang on" ... if they wished. In his case, anyhow. But he fastened his thoughts on the "hang on" and let the tail of the sentence fade out. While the clients' flame of hope was burning rather low, they nevertheless fervently believed that Mr. Shaw would pour a little more oil into their lamps.

If the secretary had some respect for the profession she would busy herself with some imitation of work. Do some filing or appear to wish to impress, since her gesture was unconsciously wounding Harry with its implication, too obvious to identify. Suffice to say, the action could be interpreted as someone who feels that the clients sitting there at the fag end of the day were not worthy or important enough to inspire in her a sense of pride. Just like a woman to make you feel that your existence posed no incitement to be on alert. The clients were of little importance to her in her scale of values. She would feel as little discomfort in front of them as undressing in front of her dog. Unfortunately, the painting of her nails dragged along the ragged nerve endings of Harry's vulnerability which said that if he were a bottle of wine, there would only be one glass left. There we sat, almost empty bottles, whereas the messenger was a rich, red ruby, ready to explode the cork out of the bottle.

"God! Get that messenger out of your mind," he ordered himself. "Stop doing that!" His bottle was nowhere near empty, for it was constantly replenishing itself. "And put an end to these negative images," he reasoned, "the girl was tired after a long day, that's all."

Now the actress who chose to ignore him, and whom he had known thirty years ago, was complaining to the man between them about the intolerable delay in getting her money from voice-overs. She spoke sotto voce lest the 'nail varnish' picked it up and transported her whine to the master. He heard her allude to the agent as a money-grabber who held onto the clients' money for as long as possible for the interest that it would accrue. The man in the middle merely nodded that he understood and sympathised, quite happy to be momentarily, but usefully, cast as a sponge for her suspicions and grief. Some people, Harry thought, can't face their past with charm, as if it bore no relation to the present, and consequently censured a whole section of their life as if it didn't exist, or if it did, belonged to an earlier character that had been eradicated. As far as she was concerned, Harry was only familiar with the one who was now dead and buried while the new one was of no concern of his. But he clearly remembered Canterbury Rep thirty years ago or more as if it were yesterday. His working periods stood out like bright stars in an infinity of blackness. Of the darkness he had no recollection, except its sameness.

But the jobs! They were conquests, battles to be fought, fears to be overcome, peaks to climb, audiences to woo, win over. Dressing rooms to entertain your visitors, champagne corks exploding into the walls on the first nights, the party on the last night, so anything connected with these voyages was highlighted in Harry's mind, and even a very casual affair stayed within his mind forever, sharply lit by the total experience. Friends stayed forever as young as they were when you worked with them, and if by chance you met such an acquaintance in the street, even thirty years later, you were apt to refer to the only universe in which you had coexisted and re-run scenes from it, enquiring after this actor or actress and how fortune had treated them. Then you might be shocked to discover that your friend has grown-up children and, in turn, these too have young ones. Then you need to rush away as swiftly as possible since they are destroying the old universe in which you live.

Everything was overshadowed by Canterbury's great Cathedral in which he had spent many an hour contemplating the martyr Thomas à Becket's horrendous end at the hands of the four knights. The play he had been in was a thriller of little renown. It had made its respectable West End run with first division players and was thus released for circulation throughout the repertory body, poisoning in the process the whole theatrical system by lowering standards and taste and losing younger audiences. Nevertheless, he had made something of the part, playing it with vigour in the echoey half-full building which, no doubt, attracted the interest of the character actress who, although also in her twenties, was more successful at playing older character bags – her face had that peculiar arch and bony set of certain

Anglo-Saxon types. During the run Harry distinctly recalled an evening of seduction, and although unable to recall exact details, traced the path from pub to restaurant to digs... It was not exactly memorable and she was not typical of the type of woman he would seek, she being more in the Agatha Christie mould and heading speedily to the Lady Bracknell school of acting. Her femininity was going through some changes, not being sufficiently in demand to keep its boilers going, and was moving through the area of barren land between the towns of male and female, not quite sure which environment might suit her best. So it had not been memorable, but it had been a raft of sorts to cling to in the dark, someone warm to hold and some sensation to feel since in those lonely Reps it was necessary to feel alive in the male sense of the word. Now, over thirty years later, she nodded; the gesture of one who lifts their head when a door opens unexpectedly. Yet they had co-mingled and, in the terms of modish vernacular, "exchanged bodily fluids." Yes, over thirty years and just worth a nod over the decades, which seemed coarsely criminal to Harry since it did not acknowledge that events in the past acquire a holiness; they are part of your history and with the pressure of years upon them your past turns to diamonds.

Harry remembered it well. Canterbury, the Cathedral, the Great Gate, chimes and tea and scones. He wanted to talk but she now indeed looked like a veritable Lady Bracknell who could not even begin to admit that decades ago her body was a receptacle for filth! She disappeared for a few moments and reappeared hooked in Shaw's arm, both smiling like Cheshire cats. As he led her to the exit he assured her in a whisper that all present could hear, since the waiting clients had stopped breathing, that "they" (whoever 'they' were) "would be delighted." Well, the gist of it was that a certain star had never been known to be off sick, so it meant a long, cosy, West End run where you merely sat in your dressing room with a book, did a couple of light understudy rehearsals a week, for the first few weeks anyway, and offered a prayer each night for the star's health with approximately the same ardour that you offered a prayer thirty years ago for some accident to happen, when you would be 'discovered.'

"And what a beautiful theatre," she added, chirping away as he closed the door on one more commission coming in weekly.

Shaw turned and faced the room wearing the same smile that he had forced onto his face for her, now being recycled for us. To flavour it up a bit he raised his eyebrow as if to share with us all the saga of the human condition – whilst life was touching it could be tiring – and so the eyebrows Morse-coded all that. Shaw's hair seemed to stand on end, as if the day's work had electrified him, and after his gesture of the eyebrows he signalled for the receptionist to go, which she did with incredible speed, and Shaw disappeared with the penultimate actor.

The neon signs of Cambridge Circus flashed their jaundiced lightning bolts across the window while Harry stared blindly out and heard the car horns squeal like pigs on the way to the slaughterhouse. The great river of working humanity was pouring out in one huge tidal flow, occasionally drowning those who hesitated, before the next tidal wave when the theatres would open their great mouths and swallow hundreds and thousands at a time, like so much plankton. On the agent's walls were posters of past productions that Harry always studied the few times he visited the office; he felt they added a degree of gravitas to his profession. The grave, bold print announced the acting legends who would be playing on a certain night. The old handbills told the bare facts with no flourish or visual ornament. Edmund Kean in *The Iron Chest* set Harry off into a reverie of chilly, foggy nights muffling the chattering sounds of carriage wheels and horse's hooves, gas-lit streets, stiff top hats, coachmen, servants, foyers crowded with a public keen with anticipation to witness young Edmund Kean at his peak. For Harry, Kean was always young and had even died at an early age. This gave him no small twinge of guilt for having passed Kean's age well over a decade ago, he blamed himself for not leaping like his idol into the turbulent river of life, risking drowning, but paddling instead in the shallower waters near the safety of the shore. He imagined Kean from the contemporary posters; bull-like neck under a dense mop of hair, arms thickly corded like those of a prize fighter. Aye, there were actors then, he mused and during these reveries, time would have a way of slowing down, the traffic ceased to flow, the horns stopped their honking and the interior of Harry's head became a film in front of which he sat, a contented spectator.

"Day dreaming?" said Shaw, as he stood there for a moment, surprised that Harry didn't leap to attention with pleasure.

"My God, I must have dozed off," Harry apologised, realising that he hadn't even seen the last client leave!

"No worries, pop in."

He walked into Shaw's small, but cosy office and,

obeying Shaw's gesture, sat down in front of the big desk which, apart from a pile of scripts, was decorated with little else except the beaming photos of Shaw's family, a happy smiling wife and two beaming offspring.

"What, must I be affronted at every step of my existence," Harry thought, as he took in the sights of well-ordered domestic life. "On every step there is some obstacle ready to send me tumbling head first down the stairs to break my neck."

It was becoming mightily tiresome. He was in a maze with ten routes all leading to destruction, yet still having to decide which direction to take, as if the decision gave you an illusion of freedom. Shaw smiled benignly, backed by further photos on the wall of past and present clients inscribed with affectionate epithets; but Harry noted with some satisfaction that there were one or two who were no longer with Shaw, but had moved to more important agencies. He began to feel better at once, since he thought he had found a chink, a way out of the maze? He was still trying to shoo those flies of sleep that were buzzing around his brain... It was very warm in there...

"Damned thermostat always breaking down, either you're freezing your bollocks off or sweating your balls off!"

Shaw smiled as if this was the wittiest thing Harry was likely to hear and anxious not to appear unfriendly, Harry grinned soppily back, lifting his head like a friendly dog had just nuzzled him under the chin. Shaw seemed so happy with Harry's response that he smiled even more, reluctant to let go of the moment with the generous curtain call that he had been given. Shaw seemed full of energy, as if the day's work had merely been some light exercise. He had happily gorged himself on the blood of others and, to Harry, he sat there like a fat bluebottle. Harry was waiting for Shaw to tell him what he had in mind for him, since the injunction to "hang on" stayed in his fantasy like a snagged thread, while "if you wish" had already been expurgated forever as if it had never existed.

Shaw began the dialogue with ... "You well?"...

"Oh yes, fine," Harry replied, adding just an *hors-d'oeuvre* of a smile to dispel any doubts about fitness, health and strength, particularly of the mental kind. "You?!"

Harry felt obliged to lob the question back, since Shaw never seemed to get old. He looked no different from the time when the actor, as a temporary measure of course, joined his agency twenty years ago after an abrupt parting from his 'first division' agent. Being with a first division agent made him feel he was swimming in a giant fish tank of exotic creatures with plenty of space to manoeuvre, enjoying a once-yearly Christmas party when he had a chance to meet some of them. Inevitably, the tanks of the smaller agents are crowded with the more common variety of fish. The agents' only hope of finding customers is the scatter-gun approach. For some years Harry swam in this overcrowded tank, deeply resenting it, yet finding it nigh impossible to make an almighty leap over the top and escape. He deeply disliked the company in which his name was placed and on chance meetings with actor friends would inwardly wince when faced with the question, "Who are you with now?" – which, of course, did not mean in your private life. It was usually the second question since the first was invariably a cheerful... "Working?"

Harry did actually manage, in the early years, to pull himself from the gravitational force of Shaw and join another up-and-coming agency that seemed anxious to retain someone of his type, but unfortunately the graft on the new agent didn't bond. It needed the blood flow of work to keep it strong and healthy and, without, it the vital tissues merely withered and died, and Harry simply fell off, like an old branch falling into a river, and drifted back to Shaw.

Shaw would always welcome him and appeared not the least bit offended by Harry's frequent attempts to escape the agent's teeming pond. In fact Shaw now made a joke after the second time, when he limply rang the agent, and quipped before he could even state his business...

"Welcome back to the fold!"

Shaw lit a cigarette, offering one to Harry which he would have liked at that particular moment, yet didn't feel it was quite appropriate to be so familiar, since he was still governed by old-fashioned values of deference to those who can in some ways affect your life.

"Well, Harry, sorry and all that to keep you so long, but wanted a tiny chatlet with you."

Harry froze inwardly for a moment and a sense of panic caused his pupils to shrink to pinpoints.

"No, no, don't let me go. Don't, no, not now, I couldn't stand it." Harry's thoughts screamed so loudly inside his skull that he was afraid Shaw's antennae would pick them up but, at the same time, would be relieved if the agent did. Shaw stared at him for a second, letting Harry swim around a little more with the shark that he had let loose before pulling him out of his misery and doubts.

"Well," said Shaw, now reeling in his line with Harry hooked gratefully from it. "It's nothing great and I could have told you on the phone, but as you happened to drop by it gave me the opportunity to say Hi, and tell you at the same time. Serendipitous! I mean you don't always want to be a voice at the end of a phone do you?"

Harry wouldn't mind as long as it was the agent's own voice answering the phone and not the obviously bored tone of the receptionist... "Sorry, he'll call you back... In a meeting... At lunch."

Sometimes Shaw did call back, reassuring Harry that he "had several irons in the fire." But Harry harboured the suspicion that Shaw never put him up for anything, and let his overflowing ghetto of actors speak for itself, like a pet shop that a potential customer idly wanders through, the more stock the better, which gives the customer the impression of vast quantities of choice.

"Children's theatre!" Shaw exploded suddenly. "A kind of new-age panto... Look..."

He saw the dismay in Harry's face as if preparing itself to receive an undeserved blow: "It's not what you deserve or should do but it's *graft*, a character heavy, and play as cast, lots of fun I'm sure, and ten weeks in Sunderland... It's not bad money either..."

Shaw thought the blow had been diverted and detected that the actor's face relaxed a tad, but it was not yet as agreeable as Shaw would have liked, and the agent did like his clients to be happy pets.

"Look," added Shaw, "I know this is not really for you, I know that and you know that, but as I said, Christmas! Why be out of work? Ten weeks, decent dosh."

"But what roles do they want me to play?" Harry was desperately trying to invest some dignity into the situation, some human and artistic decisions and not just 'panto, graft,

Christmas'... a line buzzed its way across his brain... "Let us sit upon the ground and tell sad stories of the death of Kings," but longed to substitute actors instead of kings.

Shaw, taking in one last great inhalation to stress, like an actor, a line: "Can't guarantee your roles old son, I mean it's quite usual in panto... play as cast..." Stubs out cigarette, emphatic.

Harry tried to fight back. "But good parts, good cameos, you think?"

"Well, they need a character heavy, someone versatile like you, who can switch from character to character, quick change, animal work, and I know you like... 'movement.'"

Shaw was getting tired of the sell but didn't want to lose ten weeks' commission for lack of sixty seconds more chat.

"Animal work, you mean working with animals?!" By now the interview was becoming incredulous, and a charge of anger was souping Harry's blood.

Shaw exploded with a laugh. "You must be joking old son, I mean there might be some need for animal impersonation."

"You mean like... monkeys... or lions?..." Harry tried to remember the kind of things he had seen in panto, and who knows, an animal might be a strange kind of challenge, and he was already visualising himself as an orang-utan, amusing the cast and the audience with his skills.

"Exactly, that type of thing, you may have to jump from playing an evil wizard to a monkey... or even a donkey..."

"What... you mean... get into donkey costumes, like the hind legs of a donkey?" Harry's face once again prepared itself for the blow which Shaw has to swiftly deflect, or all is lost.

"It's panto Harry, it's fun, lots of parts, twice daily, it's hard work, but it's graft and you need... the exercise... moolah in the bank. Think about it."

Shaw got up and lit another cigarette but put it immediately in the ashtray. A thin thread of yellow smoke maliciously sneaked itself into Harry's eye, as if it was an incubus serving his agent. Shaw's rising indicated that the interview was at an end and that he wished to tread another path, with his commission or not, as long as Harry *was not* on that path. Harry still sat rubbing his offended eye and hoping to savour a few more seconds of the rare audience he was having with Shaw. "Are there many lines, I mean, are there some... good roles?"

Through the window, Shaw was examining the early evening stream of people and imagining his first drink of the night at his club, but instead turned and sat back in the chair and took another longish drag, which he then funnelled out in two direct streams like vapour trails from a jet.

"Harry, it's play as cast, you take a risk but obviously they don't want to waste talent... and when I said your name they leapt on it... take my word, they won't give you rubbish. It's a fill-in, it's graft. Listen, if I had my way I'd cast you in *Lear* at the Nash but I don't, so give me a bell when you've made up your mind." Shaw now dragged the last life out of the cigarette which glowed fiercely like it might be a warning, stubbed it out, and went to get his coat on, pulled his jacket down at the back so that the collar wouldn't stick out over it, while the other hand held the collar of the top coat. He then opened the door for Harry.

There comes a point in men's lives when not to do something means that nothing is worth fighting for anymore, and when dignity is flushed down the toilet as another waste product that you do not need. Harry felt his mind toss and turn and start to unleash itself from its tether. Let it be free... let it go... his poor mind afraid to make waves. Afraid to move, fearing some terrible blow would be struck from which he could never recover... "Oh! what a noble mind is here o'erthrown..." But dignity he must at all costs save. He must speak, confess what he felt...

"Mr. Shaw, please do not dismiss me, not like this... I have been an actor for nearly forty years. For forty years I have tried to give the best of myself, the best of my being..." Harry paused for a moment and found that he had run out of breath by speaking without a break but, seeing Shaw still staring, thought it better to continue.

"I sweated my guts out, Mr. Shaw, on and off for forty fucking years, and in any other walk of life a man is respected by his peers and sets an example to his staff but in my profession, *our* profession, you have to start all over again for each job, as if you are a beginner having to audition even, and ply for work, like the forty years were as so much rubbish, yet in other businesses a man might even consider retiring at my age, be given a golden handshake and a party with many voices singing your praise, but I have to begin again and again like I'm nothing! Do you understand, Mr. Shaw, it is not only not fair, it is wretched to treat any human being like this, do you understand, it's terrible." Harry felt the power of the release, the gates were open and he felt the dew filling his lids.

"Do you know, Mr. Shaw, I have never had a night off for sickness and I've performed when I thought I was going to die, and never let the audience down? Do you know

I've played in twenty respectable theatres and acted in over, well over, one hundred plays! So please, I mean for fuck's sake, allow me one minute of your time because I have given forty fucking years of mine and that has meant sacrifices, willingly made, mind you. I mean I have no responsibilities, so I haven't got someone to come home to, waiting with the light on, but who's complaining, since I did choose my work as a calling... I love my profession, my art... that's what I chose, and so please, I mean please give me a little respect, that's all I ask; I mean I chose, I chose and love my profession and *that* is my wife and children. So why can't there be some semblance of respect in this profession, a gesture of gratitude? There isn't, is there?... At least let there be some decency between us. Let us be dignified with each other so that I feel I'm not a piece of shit to flush away, and after forty years I cannot play the hind legs of a fucking donkey, and you... *you,* Mr. Shaw, should never ever stoop or make me stoop to this!!"

Shaw merely stood at the door quietly admiring the outburst and saw in it the emotion that Harry could obviously evoke as an actor, yet seldom had the opportunity to show. At the same time, he was familiar with the crisis, as he saw one or two of these a year, and had come to regard it as the twilight of the actor, when the last real performance they are to give takes place in his office, and all you can do is let it discharge itself and fade away, leaving the client content to have made their last stand. It is a star burning itself out with one last mighty combustion before settling into tranquility and death.

Shaw gently put his arm around Harry, somewhat surprised to feel how small his shoulders were. This was the first time he had ever made physical contact with him and, for a moment, it inspired a sensation of paternalism; he used the same comforting gesture on his own children when they were hurt. He put his arm round Harry as if it could be the entire world of producers, directors and critics who had ignored and failed to appreciate the wonderful diversity of his talent. The actor felt himself melt somewhat as the heat of the agent's arm thawed the ice, and the water-filled lids overflowed down his cheeks. Shaw withdrew the arm now, feeling enough was enough, and lit a cigarette.

"I'll have that cigarette now," Harry sniffed, since this outburst had somehow equalised the position he had with Shaw, though for what reason he could not quite say, except that he now felt less self-conscious about it.

"You OK?" Shaw asked solicitously.

They left the office together, and as they walked down Charing Cross Road Harry felt different to the swirling, anonymous crowd, as if he had been released from bondage and was smelling freedom for the first time. He decided that before going home he would pop into the Salisbury Pub in St. Martin's Lane where he might venture across some actors. Shaw apologised for any unintentional slight but added that it was his duty to pass all offers over to the client, since the client can always say no. They parted at Cranbourne Street, Shaw to his stately club and Harry to his pub. There was no one there Harry knew, so he mingled a bit with the theatregoers having their pre-show tipple.

He was disappointed not to see some of his unemployed actor colleagues. The Salisbury had always been their watering hole, an oasis between the theatres of lower Charing Cross, but in recent years it had become less popular. The migratory habits of actors are indeed mysterious, and as a flock of crows will suddenly take off from one tree, only to settle on an identical one half a mile away, so it is with actors; and since Harry was not a frequent visitor to the gilded Salisbury he may have missed that migratory leap and wondered where they all were. One winter he had seen Peter O'Toole in there, standing at the bar, a Guinness in hand and looking resplendently like a leading actor, wearing a long dark blue coat with the collar up and sounding off, his crystal voice bouncing all around the pub. So whenever he visited the Salisbury and stood alone, he always recalled O'Toole standing at that precise place. Actors had certain spots where they would stand and this was right at the back which was, as it so happens, convenient for the loo and the telephone. Actors don't like to waste energy. He saw him that night, his ghost that is, looking tall, elegant and so mightily confident, a true player's player.

Thus contented with his drink, Harry allowed himself to be swept into Leicester Square Tube where he was sucked down into the abyss. He arrived home still replaying the scene in the agent's office and deriving satisfaction from it (still woozy from the one drink that had gone straight to his knees), and yet now when he played it, he linked it to the offer of work before... "But it's graft" ... I mean the donkey bit was a joke but even that can be very funny, and now he recalled his friend, Barry, telling him of the fantastic ideas they had come up with when he played the back legs in panto, which apparently brought the house down. Perhaps he had been a trifle hasty. "I mean," he reasoned, as he refilled the kettle, "it gets me away from the awful Christmas syndrome of what the hell to do, grim parties and the awful post-nuclear silence that hangs over London." And there might even be some talent up there, for even now he had not failed to acknowledge the glow he felt when in the presence of one of the opposite sex who might not be over-fussy, preferring company to nothing. So there were positive points about it and, after all, panto could be fun they say.

He was on the phone the next morning at 10am sharp, hoping and praying that Shaw hadn't offered the damn thing to anyone else. The phone was continually engaged and Harry went into a mini panic. He paced around, made continual teas which he left half-drunk, smoked an inordinate amount and continued his vigil. At last he heard the ringing tone and *yes*, the receptionist was going to put him through as soon as Shaw came off the line, and would he wait! He waited, mixing jubilation and anxiety, lest the agent at that very moment was offering his Christmas salvation to others. If only he could ask the receptionist to interrupt the call and signal his acceptance, there wouldn't even be any need to talk to Shaw. Just "Harry says yes!!" Shaw, for his part, had let access to his ear be opened for emergency cases only, such as Harry, until such time as the agent felt there was no further point. Collapsed 'stars' had a danger of turning into black holes that continually sucked your energy. If a little emergency treatment might render a service and keep the car running for a few more miles, then it's a small investment of energy. At last an anxious Harry was put though. "Hello Victor, how are you?" he began, as if to create an impression of coolness and then appear to reluctantly concede that it might be a useful fill-in over the holidays, but the agent quickly retorted...

"Changed your mind?" grasping in micro-seconds what Harry was about, as if his whole life was as transparent as glass. Of course, what else had he rung for within the first hour of the agency's opening for business?

"Bastard!" thought Harry, "OK... er yes, if it's still open."

Of course, Shaw hadn't had time to offer it around, since he somehow suspected that Harry would return to the bait and, to be quite frank, his patience with the actor wasn't purely altruistic, even though Harry's outburst did move him somewhat. It was also motivated by the base instincts of the world of commerce. Everyone else had turned it down in his agency.

"Just could you make sure I have some decent dialogue?"

"No problemo Harry, I'll tell them it's not on unless they can guarantee some substantial cameos, OK?"

"Well, errm, yes, but don't lose it."

"I'll tell them you'll take it, but make sure they give you something to get your teeth round..."

"Like a carrot?"

Shaw exploded into laughter that could be heard through his door and out to the reception area where the waiting actors all looked up, and stared at the receptionist who shrugged her shoulders.

"Harry, I think it's a good decision and it's ten weeks' graft."

"Yes."

Shaw put down the phone and in his notebook jotted down ten weeks at ten per cent and totted it up.

SUMMER SEASON

Summer Season

Yes those were the days. They were light days... not yet oppressed with the fear that over the years tended to eat away at your nerves like a slow forming rust, when the winds of anxiety battered against the windows and doors of your house and each wind carried, like a spore, a new angst that would grow inside you, insidiously, remorselessly. Yes, those were the days when you broke your comb as it snapped on your thick mane of hair and desire was ever pounding inside you, its message to be unleashed. You watched the rain pitter-patter against the window of your bedsitter and learned your lines in the grey, silky afternoons that were characteristic of towns in the Peak District of Derbyshire. In the midst of these rolling hills and rough, rugged moors lay the town of Buxton. It was a spa town, famous for its mineral waters, whose healing properties drew the old and infirm. They would gently walk through the Georgian streets and just might, after their customary early dinner, allow its digestion during a performance at the repertory theatre which began its summer season in May and ended in late September.

Harry had been selected for his youthful vitality, his looks, plus a *slight* exaggeration of his hitherto limited experience, to play what is known in theatrical jargon as juvenile lead in its weekly rep! The town's history was steeped in traditions probably going back to Roman times; a town rich in architecture, folklore and customs and much promoted, before the age of continental travel, by British

Rail, whose posters sought to advertise its charms with images of red-cheeked, bucolic lasses striding through billowing, green hills under a bright, blue sky where only one, innocent, white, puffy cloud was slowly making its way, behind which a naughty-looking sun was rising with a wink in one eye, suggesting the pleasures undreamed of to be sampled in this rather grey-haired town.

Yet now was strident youth marching with strong pulse and eager eye, learning each week another play in this sixteen week summer season. The tourists would swell the town although it was really the locals who were the loyal backbone of the audience. They would come out and cheer their favourite actors who, like the swallows, returned to gladden their hearts and entertain them once again. Two or three of the older members of the company returned year after year. These would be accorded a special ovation from an audience grateful that, after a year in which war, famine, fire and other calamities had cut its natural swathe through the world, these old stalwart thespians had survived. When they saw the actors' beaming faces make their entrance in the first play of the season, they clapped because they felt life's vicissitudes would always be overcome. It was almost with relief. If *they* returned, then everything would be alright. The Empire would survive! It mattered not that the summer season of weekly rep was considered to be on the lower scale of theatre, since it was no less popular (although a trifle coarser) than the permanent companies with their two or three weekly change of program. Weekly rep was an incredible training ground as long as you didn't do it EVERY YEAR! Ah yes, it would be nice to go to a three-weekly repertory theatre and do some Chekhov. The beauty of weekly is that the audience get to see lots of West End plays that have just come off and are still warm and vibrant from their London successes, and they can see one of these a week! Not with the West End cast of course but, as the box office lady, Mrs. Twigg, will tell you, the local rep team have been known at times to be even better! Yes, one very satisfied customer confided to Mrs. Twigg when stopping by the box office for a chat during a slack time, that the cast in *The Unexpected Guest*, an Agatha Christie favourite, was even better than when she saw it some years ago during a visit to the London sales. This reassuring information was of course passed back to the company and provided a strong sense of pride in their work, especially during the early part of the week when the houses were a trifle slim.

The season of rep was mounted each and every year by two old and crusty actor managers who had been coming to Buxton for the last twenty years. Each summer they presented their season of fifteen plays in that many weeks! They were what one might call the salt of the earth and as incorruptible as the day was long, encyclopaedic in theatrical folklore and knowledge and possessed an ability to learn their roles at incredible speed. They had created a gallery of masterpieces: irascible old colonels, cynical police inspectors, suave untrustworthy cads, funny dotty old codgers, since rep, like most theatre, was the bargain basement of literature and all human personalities reduced to simplistic stereotypes. Real live human beings were rarely seen except in the odd American drama when the whole cast would get a bit excited about who would be playing what and practising their American chewing gum accents, feeling curiously liberated in the process. Americans were more *real* than us and somehow cuter, and if one appeared in an English play, they were there to show up the inexorable reserve of the native who was somehow swept away by their brash, bold brassiness and the audience giggled sympathetically.

So Harry arrived in a particularly wet season in Buxton to play juvenile leads which meant embracing all those troublesome youths struggling with their painful, sexual awakenings and idealistic longings. They were either oversensitive neurotics in *Tea and Sympathy*, one of those real American plays; young cads in Agatha Christie going a bit bonkers which was highly fashionable for the young, bored and rich, or romantic foreigners, like Rodolpho in *A View from the Bridge.* That play was considered a 'problem play' with a message, and quite brave for the little rep to do, garnished as it was in notoriety, hinting at homosexual activity, incest and the real shocker was that it had two men kissing on stage!! ... Although forcibly done by one man to another to prove a point. Harry was destined to shine as 'Rodolpho' and these 'nuggets' made the dross of the other plays worthwhile. It was a summer season, as the agent said, for nine pounds a week. Nine glorious pounds! Harry thought. "Wonderful, ecstasy, to be actually paid for doing what one passionately wants to do, what one needs, craves, would die for. Be paid, oh blessed day ... I got the job... me!" He had, apart from some natural advantages, some experience with a touring company although he had lied about having played the lead in one of the plays that they were doing, the forementioned, *A View from the Bridge.* In fact he had been the assistant stage manager and played the small part of Louis, a 'longshoreman' whose only line was,

"Going bowling tonight, Eddie?" and had been crippled with nerves before each performance, but at least he was familiar with the play. With his reasonably attractive looks, an absolute prerequisite for the ladies, plus an insider's knowledge of their 'problem' play, Harry was their choice. "Thank you, oh thank you and bless you kind people for ever, since how was I to know that these were to be the most blessed days of my life, the most contented, even with the awful pain of learning a role a week." Some weeks the role might be a little less demanding and so one had a breather. After a couple of months of nerves, practice made him blasé and he would hardly bother to learn the last act until the Saturday morning when they would run the whole play twice.

And so on it went, like a factory or womb, bringing forth its offspring each Monday, a little runtish perhaps and undernourished, but by Friday it was a healthy, bouncing creature getting laughs and entertaining everyone. Harry felt used, alive, in demand, as each Tuesday morning they would block out the next play, and by Wednesday morning had the first act learned and rehearsed so, even after he had just seared his performance in front of an audience the night before, he was up by 10am next morning and ready to start the following one. Harry floated down the hill from his digs on a cloud of euphoria and made his way to the stage door. There, on stage, with some makeshift furniture substituting for the real thing which would be borrowed from a local furniture store in exchange for a free credit in a program and a couple of comps, he would rehearse the play. There would always be a drinks table. Most English plays had to have a drinks table as this gave the actors something to do, when writers can't quite find a way of moving their characters. After this season, the sign of a poor play in Harry's mind would be the inclusion of this object with much to-ing and fro-ing and pour-ing and 'when-ing' and the gradual drink-ing, and then the confess-ing and the refill-ing, and it's all so bor-ing.

So Harry was wrapped in work and people, clothed in words and characters, coloured in personalities like those who paint by numbers since time did not really allow more than a few brush strokes. Yet the very nature of the exercise which demanded that you be ready or else, unlocked certain doors in Harry's soul which were marked 'private, do not enter', since they contained his shameful secrets and fears. But now, caution was being thrown to the wind, the bolts drawn and light let in. Aah! fresh air at last. The fears scattered like rats but didn't move out of the neighbourhood, sensing that this might only be a temporary measure. The anonymous, lone wolf, isolated Harry, comforted in the outside world by a mere handful of friends like distant dots in a milky way, was now swimming each day in a heaving torrent of humanity. Each night the audience became a tide lapping at his feet. Each morning he asserted his position as a valuable member of the acting team, laughing with, reacting to, and helpfully showing any new young lady, brought in temporarily to swell the company, the charming town of Buxton. He was now the expert juvenile lead and the self-appointed guider of new, vulnerable, keen and eager but nervous, young flesh.

Romance was always rearing its head in Buxton, aided and abetted by those stimulating, heather-strewn hikes in the Derbyshire hills. And each afternoon there was no time for introspection or loneliness as he had to learn the next day's pages and be ready and primed, work out a few gestures and develop some bits of 'biz.' Then, after the show, the cast were thrown together in the pub opposite the theatre, an old-fashioned inn with low ceilings and passageways leading from one room to another, and where some of the audience might venture a 'well done,' all the more pleased for having seen the actor out of his mask. He would then saunter down to the Chinese restaurant with a local girl he had let get just that bit under his skin. She would wait for him in the pub. She would always be waiting for him there whenever he remembered it. She was always there and always going to be there in the endless summer season in Buxton – an eternity. The week stretched out since it carried a live thing – a play, but after a mere six performances Harry was already craving the sensation of a new experience. He'd wait for a review in the local rag which meant so much more to him then, when his name in print still gave an electric shock. So in that summer, the plays poured out of him, as if he was an instrument that the wind blew through and made music with. Other actors blended their tunes with his and they laughed together when things went wrong. On Sundays he'd relax or go for a walk with the local lass into the hills of the Peak District, where they would play at being Heathcliff and Cathy and get hungry, and sit in the same old Chinese restaurant. He felt he was existing from the top to the bottom. Yes, he was a pipe, making to his own ears the most delicious sounds.

He was a part of the town and the town was within him as the weeks slowly crawled by during the long summer between rain and shine. But now the first touches of autumn were in the air and the season was drawing to a close. In that summer he was enfolded in Buxton, soaked, absorbed, demanded, clapped, was an element of the earth, buffeted by the wind, warmed by the sun and the warm, soft limbs of his local lass, and he laughed. He laughed when things went wrong on stage. It's called 'corpsing,' although he never knew why. When did he remember laughing like that? Laughing until the very fabric of his being was in danger of disintegrating. All the rage and bitterness that had hardened into a block of ice deep within was cracking, melting and there was no stopping the flood. So he had laughed, and after the curtain came down the recollection would warm his soul again and it would start once more – the pure stream of happiness. When did I run up the moors like that with her just behind me, making compliments on my nimble feet, as if I might be a mountain satyr or a Pan sitting on a rock and playing his pipe? For yes, Harry really felt like a Pan as he lay with her in the soft and heathery moors and heard the wind whispering to them, while they sculptured the clouds with their imaginations and gave them titles. Yes, yes, yes!

That summer season seemed to last forever, and in a way it would never end, for the next year the company would be back, as surely as the swallows. Even if he was not with them ever again, he would be with them in memory as he relived that strong and unquenchable time of his urgent passionate youth. It would always stay with him, his summer season... forever.

Harry turned in his stale, solitary bed. Fifty years had passed and, in his bachelor bedsitter, he knew that the end of his own season was gradually drawing nigh and the pain would be at an end too. The rot of cancer had all but consumed him with a ferocity that was frightening, as if it wanted to get the thing over and done with as quickly as possible. It did not detect in him one of those fighters who would put up such a battle for life that the cancer would need some respite to regroup its forces. No, this victim gives himself up and shall be raided in every cell in his body, with the furious euphoria of the destroyer. However, in his dying moments, he found great tranquillity in replaying parts of his youth as if it were a memory he could feed off forever, and kept returning to that intense time in Buxton; the summer season of his youth and a merging of all seasons; the repertory season; nature's own season and Harry's own summer; the summer of his youth when his hair was dark and luxuriant as the thick foliage on the trees, and when his hot young summer spread its heat over her young female vibrancy. He stayed there in his mind and, even as the end was coming, he fixed his gaze like the needle of a compass directly into that period, as if he could then let his spirit flow back to that place where it would rest in its eternal summer season.

THE JOURNEY

The Journey

Harry found himself wandering down Charing Cross Road – it was a place to go – his legs were working on automatic pilot. He really didn't *want* to go there, but couldn't think of what *else* he could do. None of the abundant possibilities of the universe, with the million choices available to a live, sentient being, seemed to touch him – the world was suddenly shut off, and there was only one direction that he could go.

He fought the pull for a while, attempted a little wobble in the direction the current was taking him, and made some excursions along the shore. He allowed himself to be momentarily diverted by a shop window display, casting his eye over the baubles, activating his curiosity over shoes – he liked shoes. The endless possibilities of shape, form and style and why one pair seemed to touch some deep zone of desire more than another. He projected a vision of himself wearing them and was tempted to go in and ask the price. Sometimes he did this just for the five pleasurable minutes his senses were bathed in colours, shapes and the syrupy music, there to help melt your resistance. The shop was a cornucopia of delights that tempted, provoked and played with the idle mind that was adrift, unmoored, floating down a stream with no purpose – a ball of tangled weeds carried down an endless river being momentarily snagged on a bank and freed again; and then leaving the shop, not spending, not clutching another useless appendage, but free, having escaped the sirens' song. On exiting the air seemed cooler, freer, even intoxicating. You had fought a tiny battle and won. The temptations of the shop acted like a momentary narcotic, but he had escaped, and the street welcomed him again.

He wandered further afield. Was it yet time or was it still too early? Was there a right time or a wrong one? For certain things there is a right time. But now delaying tactics was the name of the game, so he took a tributary off Charing Cross and wandered into Soho. Ah, a faint but almost tangible atmosphere closed in upon him, and a different rhythm entered his steps as he penetrated another zone of time and space. He paused at a bookshop and deliberated. Yes, he could go in here. A bookshop fills you with no guilt. No time is wasted dripping through a hole in your soul. Or is Harry a boat sinking slowly into the depths of anonymity, his side wrenched open by guilt and desperation and yet vainly trying to keep afloat, cupping the water in his hands and tossing it over the side, but sinking nevertheless? No, he would float, he would navigate his way out of the doldrums. Sinking was not an option... not yet. So the books in the window captivated him. He paused to inspect the names of the authors. They were always the same authors, smiling back at him contentedly.

For a moment he would enter the shop and allow himself to drift with vague and unspecific curiosity and let his eye crawl over the thousands of books and hope there was one that would switch the light on in his mind. Yes, was there one that he might discover out of the tens of thousands that somehow held the key – he could unlock, find out, unravel the mystery – what was it? There was certainly a key. He had come near to it many a time he felt sure, but what was it? His eyes grazed the familiar titles... philosophy, biography, fiction, new age, health... somewhere between them all. He flicked open a book, a bio of some famous personality. This was easy for the unfettered mind to land on, something immediate and uncomplex, a familiar person whom one already knows in a particular way, now turned upside down. We can see the mechanics, take them to pieces, examine them and find out how it worked and whence came the key. In the beginning, in the turbulence of youth did something happen, something particular, some event that changed them irrevocably... some extraordinary metamorphosis take place whereby all the unformed, unresolved emotions and thoughts suddenly clicked into position – becoming a warrior army serving one goal – the moment of truth, the epiphany. So he thumbed the pages, took pleasure in seeing photos of the famous in their unformed youth, as young people, as Harry himself even, and then as the gaunt, strident, famous icons that we know. There was a moment. There has to have been a moment.

He closed the book and then reopened it at another place... "Shall I purchase it? Yes?" Tempted. But was it really all that interesting? He would have loved to have written a book. He thought about it and saw himself doing it. But about what? So many things would come out he was sure. Maybe it is all there... where the mystery is... where lay the key, and merely by starting, merely by taking the first steps into the deep, dark convolutions of the unconscious would the road make itself known. Just like now, allowing one's steps to be guided by instinct – not knowing what would happen – what will happen at the end... But oh, he knew but was avoiding it, making a circumnambulatory pattern like a criminal nervously surveying the object of his desire. But perhaps tonight it will change. Tonight the steps will be different, penetrating streets unfamiliar even if he has trod them ten thousand times before. Yet by a different ordering of events they will seem different – another pattern will emerge – another set of figures.

He left the warm soupy atmosphere of the bookshop where thousands of brains offered themselves and entered the streets of Soho. Soho... he even liked the absurdity of the name since it hinted at play, a land of irresponsibility, a kind of Bunyonesque symbol of roguish sin and where the weight of your vices will be lightened. A playpen, even if it had changed from the years when, as a teenager, he had wandered the streets with trepidation and awe, watching the women who draped themselves against the walls. They fascinated him and he strolled past eyeing all of them and, just for that slight frisson, just for the hell of it, would ask 'How much?' They were bored with the small minded thrill-seekers, curious eyes of the crowds who wandered into the Soho streets just for this but had to answer just in case. You had your thrill in passing them, asking them, looking at them, fantasising about them but never ever doing it... no that would be horror and misery. The asking was enough and, for that second, she was yours. How much?

"Five pounds ducky but that's on the outside."

"And how much on the inside?" and that meant for the naked immersion into the warm, soft, fissure of womanhood. That would always be a few quid more. Such women were gone. They had died years ago, but the streets were still alive with their ghosts. Harry remembered them and placed them back there where they belonged against the walls.

It somehow reassured Harry to resurrect Soho in its old setting as if this was of vital importance to solve the mystery that was haunting him. He was a detective at the crime scene, restaging all the events just as they had happened, in the hope that something would leap out of the unconscious memory that could not be triggered otherwise.

The evening was slowly darkening and the streets were filled with workers who, in Harry's mind, had sacrificed their energy, brains and skills and were now rewarded with the sharp, fresh air of freedom. Freedom was the desire that Harry craved above all, above everything, above all sensation, freedom, but that only comes after a trial of strength and endurance. The sweet pang of freedom. The curtain down. The applause. The arduous, heart-thumping test... the exposure... the conquering of fear... the end. The street after the event. The rush of cool air on your skin. The sweet smell of freedom. The burning up of all human endeavour in the act of work! How he envied even the office workers as they shot out of the buildings, bundles of energy anticipating the night's rewards with every pore of their body. Freedom meant hunger, taste, thirst, desires, plans, all with the precious hours of liberation. How to divide those hours into segments, each segment a reward for having sacrificed your energy which would then would be renewed as a reservoir renewed by rain. The enthusiasm! Each had their fantasy of what they would do with their golden hours of freedom. Harry had *only* freedom and therefore had none and each moment of freedom was a tiny whip lashing him, was a minute of guilt, was a heavy minute that weighed heavily upon him. A brain longing to be used. A dog, tethered and wearying, waiting. But soon,

soon, it will be soon. I am sure it will be soon. Hath not the agent said it will be soon. Yeah, they, them, the others, those, the powers that be, the almighty, were making up their minds.

"You were perfect for it. They definitely wanted you, Harry, you Harry... you were their choice, they liked you, oh yes, BUT were making up their minds, yes they did like you for the part... No I swear, would I lie to you? What for?"

"But why are they taking so long?"

"Who can tell these things?"

"Aren't they worried that I might get another job?" (Unlikely as that may seem.)

"Well that's the risk they're prepared to take, but soon it will be soon. If I don't hear by next Monday *I'll* call *them.*"

Harry paused as he passed Chinatown. It felt as though he was in China. The streets were busy with the frenzy of restaurants getting ready for the night. All Chinese. Nothing left of the streets that he knew as a teenager when the whores leaned against the walls. He saw them from the small office where he worked in Gerrard Street.

And so he passed his old office building and thought he glimpsed his fifteen year old frame, or rather his ghost, enter the building – ah yes, he was retracing his steps – he was seeking to unravel the ball of string that would take him back to some moment in time. Or was he just drifting on the past, floating on his back on the Dead Sea of ancient memories. No, there was a reason, in the scheme of things a reason will emerge. The clues are there and, like Sherlock Holmes, he will find the answer by carefully examining the evidence but; unlike Sherlock, he doesn't know what he is looking for... not yet... but will. It is there... somewhere... there. In Soho? Not necessarily, but maybe. Maybe it is. But Harry *knows* that it is... knows in the back of his mind that it is... will be... inevitably... "Don't dodge the issue." "But I'm not," he thought. Harry liked these ping-pong games with himself and as soon as a negative thought was served, he would smash it back with a positive one; the same in reverse, bouncing his thoughts back and forth. "But for now something is leading me..." there is a reason behind every action. Perhaps he will unweave the wool and come to the place where the stitch went wrong, and from that wrong move everything following became distorted, more and more awry. His ghost disappeared from the office and now the Chinese restaurant was filling with people ordering the exotic things that he had no appetite for. He watched them trampling over his youth... his memories... The brown, roasted corpses of animals hung in the window. Harry surmised that they were suckling pigs flattened out by a steam roller, and these were meant to tempt you in! As he stared at the lean face of the chef working behind the window, furiously chopping and cutting, a sliver of envy ran through him. The chef's face was bundled into a convolution of muscles as he single-mindedly pursued his craft. Harry knew that the chef's mind couldn't wander, drift, but was anchored, determined, focused. The chef caught Harry's eye for a moment and he felt a twinge, as if his unemployed uselessness could be detected by him whose energy was flying out like sparks from a hammer. A spark illuminated Harry for an instant and then was gone.

Soon... it will be soon. Soon his energy will too be set on fire, raging, burning, an inferno as he detonates the text, swallows the words up whole like fuel, like the paraffin that street performers hold in their mouths and then spew out in a tongue of flame. That's how it will be. I am sure of it, he thought. I am. Hath not the agent said so. "Yea from the tables of my memory I will wipe away all trivial fond records... and thy commandment all alone shall live... unmixed with baser matter, yes, by heaven!" Some of Shakespeare's lines flew into his brain or emanated from there for no particular reason. Perhaps triggered by something... giving him a shot of inspiration, a bolt from the blue. Was he now too old to play Hamlet? Not in Harry's mind, no, not so. In his heart he would never be too old. The role sang through his spirit... awakened him when he was tired, forlorn, depressed. Suddenly, eureka! Hamlet would shake him, fire him up... Yes, Hamlet the Dane was gripping hold of Harry, inspiring him with his passion. There for every mood. Even in Harry's most soulful moments he would be there to sympathise and cajole... "How all occasions do inform against me..." to "what a rogue and peasant slave am I," when deeply frustrated, or "bloody bawdy villain," when downright furious, and "what a piece of work is man," when feeling sanguine or poetic. So now Harry continued his journey, his sails being momentarily filled with little gusts of Hamlet. Yes, and even now his blood started to warm. He felt the words tingling his flesh and arousing his spirit. This is what drama is... it is the embodiment of another spirit. He comes when he is needed. Harry crossed Shaftesbury Avenue mouthing Hamlet, silently moving only his lips... taking sustenance from the words... fuelling himself on them... a mantra. He took a sidelong glance at passers-by lest they should mistakenly interpret the rehearsing thespian as a lonely misfit talking to himself.

Now the sky was darkening, the lights were coming on and now the weight was easing off his back... even in the walking he was shedding the weight of his moral responsibility. Now the workers had left the offices and were unemployed like he. Now the acting agencies were closed and so there were no calls being made and no offers were coming in for other actors. Ah, at last some respite... even his agent sitting there bloated, grinning, always happy, always engaged, seemed to threaten him as he sat on a vast dunghill of offers that were not destined for Harry; but now nobody is being offered anything and the agency is closed. He does not have to phone, does not even have to resist the painful desire to phone. Does not have to look at the instrument and will himself *not* to phone. Does not have to torture himself by having phoned and having phoned and left a frustrated message, then be suffused with anguish for having made it. Now all is at peace. The day with its turmoil was coming to an end and the end was in sight. The goal. The finale. The ultimate quest to wherever his legs were leading him, like a moth to the flame, fluttering, fainting and weaving, soaring and diving but leading it there. Inevitably.

Now the Dane's words were swimming round his skull, freeing him, a drug, unloosening the great creaking barge of debris and letting him sail aided by strong gusts of *Hamlet.* As he walked he almost wished he could shout the words out just once. A big yell... Those great wonderful explosive moments when the latch bursts open... "My fate cries out and makes each petty artery in this body as hardy as the

Nemean lion's nerve" Harry wanted to shout it out, to hurl it from him, to expectorate his venom on Hamlet's words but had to be content to let it ring and bounce around his skull. Almost wished he was back in his room so that he could vent it loud and clear.

He looked at the workers darting through the streets, while some had attached themselves to little pavement cafés and were happily crushed together, drinking cappuccino and yacking about their day. Fortified by his boost of *Hamlet*, his envy of the workers evaporated. Now they seemed insignificant to him, wallowing like pigs in the simple effluvium of their nightly escapism... dribbling their low life experiences and tatty adventures, lighting cigarettes, munching old croissants, laughing, talking and waiting for nothing. His excoriation of them was probably no more than a delayed reaction for having envied them earlier; pre-*Hamlet*. They can never play Hamlet – never. But he, yes he, Harry could, and would, and shall, and even now is. Somehow Hamlet seizing Harry or Harry seizing Hamlet had placed him even temporarily on a higher plane of existence and he was seeing the world through *his* eyes, through the sharp but delicate prism of *Hamlet*. Through the heightened, coruscating vision of the Dane and was happily floating above the throng.

He felt himself pulled in the direction of a certain restaurant that was, many years ago, the scene of a celebratory dinner after the last performance of a play that he had made no small success in. He stood outside the restaurant and waited for the memories to come flooding back. They inevitably did, not just now but always, since he was always trying to capture the moment, not in the familiar way we tap into the nostalgia of past pleasures but with the zeal of a detective searching in the mud for clues. As he stood staring longingly at the past, Hamlet flew off, departed, was gone, fled, and the old feelings of remorse and yearning took its place. He saw himself drinking champagne celebrating a triumphant ending. He had thought all this out before, but were there some elements in the picture he had glossed over?

"GO BACK. Remember... can you remember the applause at the end? No, not quite, not really recall that. Not recall the *leaving* of the theatre, packing up and taking all those things... but remember the dinner and that was a good one." There were just the four of them and for once... yes, that once, he was the champion of his fate.

He saw himself through the window celebrating with his friends at the once famous restaurant. His spirit was aflame then, his body filled with pure ether, purged and purified, but now others were sitting at his table weaving their memories over his. The restaurant was renowned in the past and had a glorious history where Oscar Wilde had entertained his young friends, but now it had lost its reputation in pursuit of the common man where easier and less discriminatory money was to be made... easier the present owners thought, than competing with the Olympians of culinary art. Like Harry, its fortunes had waned but he had known it when both shared the glory. He had belonged then. Then. He passed by, the memory trailing after him for a while, a wisp of smoke and then fading out.

Now he was allowing his feet to work out some pattern, some complex formula, one that would lead to some conclusion that had not occurred to him at the beginning of the journey. His feet might belong to another Harry, a younger Harry who would guide him, yes, actually lead him to a solution which the old Harry could not conceive. The young man was trying to show him the way! He was a hypnotist, gently leading the subject to a buried treasure that the older man had almost forgotten, one that could not be detected through the noise of the conscious mind. So Harry let himself be led and blindly followed his feet. Or was he really fooling himself since he knew his destination well enough, knew it as a swallow knows by instinct where it must head, and flies on trusting its innate knowledge to lead it to a sanctuary where it will thrive and be safe. Its wings just obey a mote of memory and fly blindly on. So does Harry really know where he is going but pretends not to, or perhaps hopes that this time there may be another solution... another destination. Not in this warren of streets but in time and space. Another time. So the steps are charting memories until the clue is found. The answer will be found!

Again he allowed his feet to go whither they wished and came unto a crossroad, a main artery running across Soho and strolled into it. He looked up. Yes, there was a flat on the top floor of a building he had once visited. He had in times past left part of himself there. Yes, there was another mark, as if he were a wanderer in some vast forest who diligently scored a small nick in the trees so as to provide the clues to his exit and now was slowly, but definitely, finding his way out. Her name was Annie and he was up there with her in the flat – his youth was there, still there in turbulence and desire. Still seeking and imagining a vast and unseeable future that had the enormous potential of mystery. Was it during one summer? It always seemed to be summer then and Soho was alive and bursting, a ripe fruit in Berwick Street market, the old market that ran down the side of the street. That's where he would shop for bargains when the avocados were soft and bruised and therefore cheap; and so he would buy them and bring them back to Annie. He had to pick up the threads and somehow link them together. If he could link them then perhaps a current would flow through and illuminate everything. All would be seen. Then.

He had slept many nights in Soho. Slept and was comforted by she who passed through his life and was part of it. Then the thread snapped! Why? He could not remember the ending, only the fading out. So he was drawn to the source of this life-force, or where his life had been for several moments in history charged. Alive! Ah, so there it was. Moments in time that he himself had illuminated... switched on... was a current... a current of *aliveness*. So he was re-seeking these points in time as if Harry, the actor, was merely an instrument that was not dead, but inanimate until he plugged himself into a source, and came to life! There it was. So Annie had been a source to experience aliveness. One of the sources, and since she enabled him to feel the wonderful sensation of existence, powerfully and completely it had stayed in his memory and now he had sought it out. His feet sought it out. He was like the swallow, seeking sustenance and sanctuary yes, just like the little swallow. But the source had gone. His feet were pursuing shadows. A dog returning to its old bone that had been stripped clean. But the memory of sustenance lingers and he would find sustenance this night. But the clues. They became stronger. Woman. The women were a source of this sustenance in which he could escape, and not only escape, which seems like running from something, but escape through joy, feeling alive, lit up. But yes, running from something. The pitiful emptiness, the vacancy, the absence of the text, the work, the power and the fulfilment of his life's gift. So they had been an escape... a plunging into... a return to... a longing and a yearning for, since they, the women will not reject you, not yet... will not cast you off... will not judge and ignore you, but offer themselves as comfort and warmth, as flesh and spirit. A harbour, a sanctuary. But as time took its toll, as time does... then the sanctuary becomes harder... harder to find... as time passes the journey is harder. As time passes the sanctuary becomes a wall... as time passes what you have to offer them becomes less desirable... as time passes, so does it pass for them, and the escaping, the plunging, the bathing, the burning of energy is replaced by an interweaving of souls. That begins with desire and stays when desire wanes. Love can remain even when the flesh has gone. Soul mate. So there it was. Yes. It had ended before the interweaving had taken place, had begun, and he had pulled away from it leaving torn threads... which he now sought to rejoin... foolish thought. But. Why? Each time starting again and yet again. Always. A pattern there. As time passes partners need an interweaving of souls; but you, yes you, pulled your soul away. Why? The clues were now falling like the rain that was beginning to lightly fall onto the narrow Soho streets and those at the little outside tables drinking cappuccino were now scurrying to find places inside.

Soon it will be time but not yet. Not quite yet, for he had not quenched his thirst for memories. There was still more – still more places he could touch and see himself arise in all his glorious, flaming youth... a genie from a lamp. He wondered where Annie was now, smiling so sweetly in his memory. There forever. That gentle, wistful smile. The corners of the mouth turning up at the end, believing she didn't quite deserve the pleasure, but allowing the lips a little uplift. So that was good. That was fulfilling, but that soon faded back into the deep folds of memory as his feet continued, on and on, the smell of the past fading... and still watching, waiting for the clues. Oh how many times he has done this and not found it, but now, even now he was getting warmer... yes he felt a glow suffuse him, a tingling, a moving, a sensation working its way through his body. Yes, he felt something different this time. It pricked his eyes. They felt moist. He wanted to cry but tightened his jaw instead, and held the tears at bay but even that was good. Felt alive – yes he would cry but not now, not in the street at least. FELT, and that was good – was that not at least alive? His feet paused by an old coffee shop he used to frequent in the distant past. The place was packed as always, and you'd think there was no other place to go, so popular it was with students from the local art school. Should he go in? No, that time had passed when merely walking in there filled him with pleasure. The croissants were always large and crusty. Through a door at the back there was a phone where you could call your agent. He suddenly remembered the phone. For some reason now he remembered it. Oh yes, it hit him, – yes of course. His feet knew what he did not. It was here, oh God here. How could he have forgotten? Was it not here in this simple coffee shop that he celebrated his marriage? Here. A celebration of coffee and croissants. So there we sat after the ceremony in the registry office and consummated our marriage with patisserie. And so he searched his mind to find her there. Will she not always be there? Happy... yes, we were joyful that day and thus began a co-mingling of souls... so there was in his life an interweaving of those thousands of strands until the tapestry is made. But then. Ah then! The loosening, the pulling away, the tearing, the desire, the escape again. But there she was. She was. Always a was. On and no more of this! So Harry moved away picking up the loose threads and once more crossed Shaftesbury Avenue, the rain quickening his steps. Past youth, past success, past loves, past friends, past joys, past.

He was now taking charge of his feet – now thinking on his feet, since his feet had only led him into misery and regret; but the clues were there and he was grateful for that... something had certainly been unlocked and it was up to him to peer inside – yes it was there and all he had to do was be unafraid and seek it out. But not now. Now was enough. Now his destination was becoming apparent as he crossed Charing Cross Road once more and headed into an alley lined with second hand bric-a-brac and bookshops full of the dusty tomes of yesteryear. He liked these bookshops. They too were repositories of memories. He liked thumbing through old biographies of the great actors in the period when they reigned in their temples, the theatre and wished he could climb those steep slopes and join them. The great actors were aloof – on pinnacles – on icy wastes – alone, gaunt, brave and manfully dying for their art, dying near the stage if not actually on it. Dying in another actor's arms. He examined a print of one, depicted with a leg slightly crooked, the body leaning back as if taking on all that fate could throw at him. Harry had tried to climb those icy slopes, had clawed at them but somehow slid down into the unknown masses at the base, joining those struggling and climbing over each other... maggots in a fisherman's tin box. So he looked up to them and saw them in his mind's eye as the statues you might discover in parks of great men looking eternally and everlastingly noble; chiselled, and undisturbed by a pigeon squatting on their heads. So through the books he came close to his dead idols. He lived through them and travelled on journeys with them, shared their failures and their suffering, ignominy or neglect, certainly shared that, but when that moment came! That great moment when time and space came together and they were in the centre and good fortune smiled, then Harry smiled with them. Their suffering and endurance had equipped them all the more to be ready when the time came. Harry was ready for he too had traced a similar journey, but his time was to come. Yes, his time would come. Soon.

Now he came to the end of the alleyway and saw the audiences entering the theatres. He turned into St Martin's Lane. There was no other place to go. Now this is where his feet had led him, unwillingly at first. Had tried to divert him... had tried to show examples of the past, had tried to take him back, had tried to retrace his steps so that he might set his feet on a new path... not go back to the old one... not again that one... so this was the clue. It had arrived without knowing the crime. He had not known of what he was guilty but still attempted to find the clues to solve the crime. Ah the clues. They were there and provided the answer. "But yes, once I have the answer, once I know what the answer is, might that just be too horrible to contemplate? To know the *truth*. Would that be just too awful to see? To see what you really are? Not what your fantasy has shielded you from, the way a perfume masks your real, essential self. Could you bear it, could you? Could you see yourself as perhaps not being such a very talented actor after all, and that rejection was not part of some mysterious conspiracy against your special and unique gifts, but based on purely what you have to offer? Can you bear to see your image in that mirror? And that the sacrifices you have made of the simple pleasures and sustenance of life and love and interweaving was for a chimera? Because if you are not an actor then what has all the suffering been for? And who and what are you? *That* you will see – blinding searing truth! But truth also purges and gives strength eventually – a foundation to build on. Not quicksand, but stone. Not yet... no, not yet... not just yet. I'm not even sure if that is what I'm looking for," he thought. "I still have faith. The agent *will* call by Monday, he did say that."

He paused for a moment to peer through the patterned window of the pub. It looked cosy and perhaps he would find mates in there, colleagues, acquaintances. Anyone. But here he could burn up his energy. Here he could ignite his spirit. Here he could plunge his soul into the warm bath of alcohol... here he could drown his soul, or at least put it to sleep for a while. Stop its howling. Numb it. And so he entered the pub known at one time as being a haven for actors. This is where his feet had led him albeit reluctantly. I wish there was another ending dear God, I wish. He ordered his drink. After a couple of hours all was quiet within his soul. Quiet.

AGENT

Agent

He woke up in the same state as he had gone to bed, thinking about it, worrying, agitated. Had the explosion set off a series of echoes around the agency? He couldn't keep it in. It had soured his mouth, curdled his stomach until he was carrying pure acid that eventually detonated, spurted in a stream of frustration down the tube and into the waxen ear of the dumb tart who worked for Max. 'Max' being the geek into whose grubby hands he had laid his precious life – his agent. So he hoped to get to him through her, that she, as an appendix, would absorb the poisons of Harry's body while the agent would be spared. She would take the blows while the master felt only the reverberations. You don't want to smash the relationship by the impact of your angst, so you need a punch bag. A good secretary knows this only too well and absorbs your anger, sensing that its lavorial flow is not really meant for her, and remaining oblivious to it while the client vents. A sister of mercy. He counted on her feminine shrewdness, her natural ability to filter male wrath, to reinterpret the vituperation, the spleen and the bile as passionate concern from an emotional actor. After all what is an actor without emotion? A tasteless fruit.

She was a Desdemona that he would use as a bridge to reach Othello, except this was no Othello. This was a poisonous toad who sat on people's fates; who darted round the city, a rat gathering refuse from the garbage bins of film studios and then dividing it amongst his clients.

If you were one of them you might sup at the table, but should you fall out of favour or fashion, then you would be kept in a distant cage in a remote region of their minds and let out when the 'scraps' came in: weirdo parts, psychopathic killers, rapists, cold-blooded Nazis, and of course sadists. Thus had the agency in their mind-set reduced this actor's vast comedic and tragic abilities to the elements suitable for Hollywood mulch, ergo if you could play Macbeth, Malvolio or Richard III, it followed that your talents were more suitable for loonies and the deranged. Most films had little space for such quixotic creatures as actors. Characters were now divided into two archetypes in the Hollywood lexicon; 'good guys,' or 'bad guys.' Film plots had no need for the wide range of emotion, or the extraordinary spectrum of human experience that Shakespeare would use to colour his vast canvases. These days, there are few equivalent movies needing such a chromatic range, so everything is reduced to primary colours. The complex type of personality needed to fuel the classics was the driving force of the 'bad guys,' the criminals, as any complexity in human nature suggested derangement... Thus film in its simple-minded way embraced the attitudes of the extreme Right that divided the world into good and evil. As Shakespeare's weapons were the verse, the soliloquy in which man or woman defined themselves, by the mordant wit, the brilliant epigram, so film's weapon was the gun. It would severely strain their imagination to make a film without one.

However, as civilisation edges towards its decline, and Harry with it, the constant percussion of his fears and doubts wouldn't stop, would not let off. For, even if he only played simple-minded guys for the rest of his life, he would at least try to endow them with a vestige of human colour. But would he even be suggested for such roles? He hadn't heard from his agent in six weeks! He had forgotten how to smile during this time for he construed that this silence must be saying something that he does not want to hear. Six weeks! And no returned call. The percussion kept its rhythmic beat and would not let off, would not let him enjoy food, drink, love, light, air, people, as it beat away constantly, an obsessional drumming. Neglect was one of the beats, a steady downbeat, insistent, keeping the other beats in some kind of order as they weaved in and out the main driving thwack that smashed the message over and over again. Neglect! Oh infamous, but then in counter-beat and with no less insistence was the alternate rhythm of isolation – from the agency, from the others, the elite team which Harry would love to be in, to be a member of that club. True, he was seldom employed; true, he had had no job through them in three years, but at least he could be called for an availability check! A dreadful word! Are actors a commodity, in stock or temporarily unavailable, that anyone can buy? Still, he had the hallmark of the agency on the reverse side of his photo, IFA, International Famous Actors. To him that was a stamp, evidence that he was at least worth some carats, a validation of the purity of his metal. With the mark of IFA, people would read on and study your cv, not cast it into the waste bin of the great unknowns. It was a club that gave you *power* by association (even if you didn't work).

"I was part of that club where the great ones, the great knights, had resided no matter if that was in the distant past and they were there in their dotage. Nevertheless some tiny drops of glory must trickle down to me," he mused, and if there was a danger that he would be extirpated, ripped out, pulled out by the rude hands of a gardener and thrown upon the compost heap like some inferior plant, then his life would lose all colour and meaning. This club is exclusive, hard to get in, but once in you had the possibility of being catapulted to fame and landing in the safety net of perpetual work or, equally, of being totally neglected. The agency was really a kind of factory shaping the actors of the future, those who could fulfil the traits of the modern hero, thus satisfying the young audience's hunger for their mirror image. Rebels, brats, louts, yobbos who barely spoke English, attractive hooligans, or ex-models were the new grist.

No matter how he tried to reconcile himself to his plight with the disdain that he had for these creatures, the self-accusing beat was a stronger thwack. Yes, the neglect beat was stronger, and then the other beats, a thousand others, a great Brazilian batteria of beats, disgrace, ignominy, anger, fear, loneliness, rejection, jealousy, envy, hate and exile. But where to now? Actually, those not suffering the ravages of struggle that the years had worn into Harry, this desperation and obsessional drive, might have decided very coolly to go to another agency, who also might have appreciated him. But, to the compulsively afflicted, symbols carry a greater weight than reality. He could not bear the magic symbols of IFA to be struck from his page. The beats continued, grew stronger as the force of his imagination added surreal ingredients to the rhythm. Sometimes the beats would ease off; some he could drown out and some he could distract; some he could reason away, but the big one always made its incessant and predictable thump. Neglect. He was neglected. That much was certain. Harry could not understand that the neglect was the bitter fruit he had to bite if he wished to stay on the agency's tree, for the sun now shone on the glitter, the trash, on those who brought in the shekels. He could not fully understand this, possessing the actor's predilection for sitting on the scales of self-worth, constantly weighing his value – a gold standard – one day up, the next depressingly down, never constant. Being such a fluctuating commodity gave him little time to rest or view the work situation objectively. He only saw more and more attention and care lavished into the opposing scale which grew heavy with riches and glory as his lighter one soared upwards.

He had few friends, more like acquaintances, who also inhabited the same club, and he worried about how his relationship with them might change, and gradually die off. He'd be marooned in space. He wondered at their successes and heard about them regularly flying off to LAX, where long, black limos would pick them up as if they were precious and rare animals to be pampered. They'd return, their pockets stuffed with big cheques while, at the same time, exchanging stories of cynical disdain, yet secretly craving, needing, loving, hogging and wanting more, much more, of the same. *Please!* Yes, they loved Hollywood, and their occasional smug picture in Vanity Fair. They loved to go to the town that shits out movies, and be embedded in them like pieces of gold or precious gems, glittering in the darkened wombs of the cinema. The agents sat licking their chops and congratulating their clients on their small supporting performances, debating them to death in the latest trendy watering hole, while waiting for the next crap, courtesy of LAX.

So, anguish produced its perpetual throb without end, a curious and incredible syncopation, while other thoughts produced wild fugues. Or they were viruses that constantly multiply and as reason smashed one on the head, like a deadly plague they developed even more insidiously. They took on spectral proportions. To the secretary, who runs backwards and forwards like a dog attending to its master's needs, he addressed the fusillade of his thoughts... "For God's sake, it's not too much to ask, some human fucking response, Penny! I'm his client. I think he'll remember me. (Sarcasm was an outlet.) Yes, I know you're not to blame, Penny. Yes, yes, I do know that. I'm not blaming you but it's his job to *communicate*, I mean we are in the communication business. I'm sorry I swore. It's just so damn frustrating. Yes, I know he was in Cannes... that was a week ago. Oh, please don't give me that *crap.* I have a life I entrusted to him, my valuable, complex human mind!... Do you understand what I'm saying?!"

Or words to that effect. And after he made a cup of tea, he felt good, good to have squirted the venom out of his jaws. Felt whole again, complete, honest in his soul. But, as it so happens, one cannot always survive according to one's beliefs and values twenty-four hours a day and a doubt came slowly swimming into his mind; a slow moving shark was just drifting in on the sea of his doubt and seeking out some vulnerable part. Fear was creeping slowly in and, as the heat of the adrenalin wore off, the shark moved in on the rudderless Harry, marooned as he floats out on the infinite waters. The fear was triggered by the little bubble of anxiety that came floating to the surface of Harry's mind and it concerned Penny. Would the Woolworths name possess a Woolworths mind, a cheap, functional, plasticky, ordinary, plain, useful, tidy dish-mop that would wipe things up? Or would she have a Penelope mind that was cunning and astute, understanding the fragile temperament of actors and 'interpret' the *petit mal*, even reshape it to give it form and elegance. Is she not sensitive to the frustrations of the thespian? "Harry's suffering a little pique, some understandable concern over what he perceives to be less communication than he would like!" Yes, something like that, or was the reality...

"Harry rang again, Max."

"Oh no!!"

"Yes, it's the fifth time this week and all he did was scream down the phone... He was having a fit!"

"Ooh God."

"Acting like a lunatic, shouting and swearing at me, like I was to blame."

"What a loony, Jesus!"

"He was crazy."

"Oh he's crazy alright."

"I mean what did he get at me for, why shout and screech at me? I think he's going bonkers."

"Yeah, he's going nutty in his old age, maybe we should let him go."

Yes, I am sure she's human enough to understand and not be a twerp and quote me verbatim. I mean actors are like that. She must have had lots of calls exactly like that and knows how to field them. But six weeks! He then thought it out in the most creative way he could – this enabled him to do something about it (the nagging thoughts were like leeches clinging to his flesh). So Harry would forget that they were agent and client and write a letter hoping to invoke his humanity. No attacks, no accusations or complaints, just a simple and moving epistle of frankness. Yes, he would bare his heart.

"Dear Max, you know, once I was considered a great actor" – no, strike that... "a very good actor" – no, that's too soft... "an actor of great promise" – no, that's too youthful; something more of a confessional about life and times, the difficulties, the strains, the hopes and how basically we *need each other*, as brothers, comrades, that we should speak more, have a glass of wine together, talk about our aspirations, our dreams, share them, like a picnic, how we all inhabit a small world and we people this little world. That at the moment I could be Richard II in his solitary cell, trying to fill my world with thoughts that are ever breeding and in the morning, as I wake, they fly to me and hover like a swarm of bees. Speak to me beyond films. You didn't call back. "I was in Cannes" crap. Of course, having an idiot for an assistant doesn't help those craving the warm milk of human affection. A clever woman could assuage and pacify and be a link to you, so that we might feel your touch through her. However, enough of that. Just be a little human, gentle, kind, caring, loving, understanding and build a stronger bridge between us instead of the yawning gulf...

So Harry thought of penning such a letter, but something in him knew that this was a bitter, cynical age and such emotional gestures might be construed as begging, cringing, and even more loopy than the shouting. For him there was something in it that felt distinctly correct – it was the unexpected way, the way he performed, never taking the usual route, but straight to the bone. Yet he feared, above all, the mockery. For what can swine make of pearls? The agency was a factory for the face that fits, the type, sex, and forget about acting for now. He might not even have time to read your pleas, but there it was, taking root in his mind, waiting to be born.

OK, this is one side of Harry's fertile brain, the grovelling, pleading bare-all side, but the reverse was dedicated to fantasy. He would close them down, would invoke the sympathy of his union for various abuses for betraying the articles upon which any agency is allowed to perform its duty, i.e. blackmail. The agency might, as was widely rumoured, hold a film company to ransom by giving them a star so long as they took a few of the agency's 'faves' as well, some also-rans: putting together deals called 'packaging' whereby they are also acting, not as agents, but as producers. They become a kind of employer and there are laws governing the conduct of agents. Breach of such laws renders them unfit for the office of the guardian of human souls. He felt a little better for his momentary mental act of rebellion since his dramas were always rehearsed but seldom, if ever, performed. They wish to lop him off the tree but haven't got the guts, the human gumption, the decency to say it, but expect that by their silence, the low ethics of the yellow, gutless coward, to signal it to the actor for whom trust is all he has to believe in. So he invests this commodity, trust, in this keeper and finds that his cup of trust is spat in and used to damp out dog-ends. Silence, only silence, and each day's silence adds weight to the day before and you, Harry, are expected to construe in this silence a message saying, "we have no need of your services nor feel we can help you in any way," that's what it is meant to say. But it also says "The pool is overfull and we have the bargaining power... you haven't earned a penny for us in years and each second you take speaking to and abusing our secretaries costs money... in *fact* you are a liability... in *fact* you don't even merit the cost of a letter and because I am the sleaze king of agents I can do anything. Morality, ethics, values, human decency doesn't rule, effect or guide me, merely the market and you are worthless to me and to us. So take off."

That's what Harry thought and each day, each hour the pain of the drum beating into his brain was beginning to concuss him... if only it didn't matter so much. Why did it? Surely he might find another agent who respected his artistry. He had often considered it. Was it the rejection itself that pained? Were the roots long and deep and did they lead to a father who neglected him as a youth, poured contempt on his head and scorn at his attempts to become what he did become, an actor. So he also carried that particular virus, a dormant rogue that could be activated when it heard the familiar drum beat. What did they call it? Conditioned reflex?

Next day he sat down, made a list of other leading managements he would not be ashamed to be with and rang them one at a time, but the replies were curiously similar. They said they admired his work but unfortunately their books were full, adding that it wouldn't be fair to him to take on someone and not be able to give them the kind of sensitive handling and time they deserved. Thus the perfect kiss-off, flattering you while giving you the boot! He even thought of raking up old embers of agents who had helped him in the past, although he had used them as rungs to the next tier until, one day, he broke through the dull cloud of mediocre agents and saw, for the first time, the pinnacle where lived the great agents: those agents you seldom see and by whom your calls are seldom returned, except through their underlings, sometimes not even that, but at least you are a member! Of course the chiefs are too busy to return your calls. They live like the legendary bird on the air, making calls from supersonic jets to their starry clients in detoxification clinics; and when they do land it is only to glide over the polished hardwood floor of the Ivy Restaurant. Here they might, should you also be there after a performance (wouldn't dream of being seen there if unemployed), catch a glance from your upturned face, which shines like a spotlight on the agent's entrance. The agent returns the acknowledgement with no more than a slight narrowing of the eyes, a meagre pursing of the lips, enough to let you know that they've IDENTIFIED YOU AS A CLIENT!

However after a week of phoning, and polite, respectful rejections with the usual excuses, Harry came to the conclusion that, although he believed his talents were indeed unique, exceptional and original, they were not for this quotidian world of predictable roles and simplistic characterisations, and he was not going to crawl to the third division agents from whence he had begun his arduous climb upwards thirty years ago. No, that would be too ignominious, to have his name in the actors directory in which your credits are writ, under a third-class agent, thus suggesting by implication that you, Harry, were a *third-class actor*! No, never give that wretched twerp, Penny, whose value was even less than the name that so suited her, never give her the satisfaction (oh that dumb sneer she wears on her face) of gleefully pointing out to her boss, your ex-agent, your demotion.

There was one agent left who, he had no doubt, would accept his gifts and who he had at various times in the past considered, but never felt quite ready or even worthy for that matter. Now he was considering the possibility once again and, whereas before it was pure fantasy, a self dramatisation, circumstances were now gently nudging him to a more realistic solution. He was out on a plank being pushed, albeit gradually, and he could look down and see the waves far below, and the writhing tormented limbs of the unemployed actors drowning in the agonies of their frustration, or exhausted, swimming from rock to rock, seeking solace and small jobs and then being washed away by the sheer force of the mass behind them. Some luckier members of the new wave might cling to a rock, blink for a while in relief, having found a temporary sanctuary, but another giant wave is already behind them, ready to topple them and repeat the process.

Was Harry ready to jump back into that throng and eke out a life as a player of bits and pieces, the odd 'telly' and a spot of teaching young louts at a third rate drama school, whose interest in the art of classical speech was minimal compared to their daily fantasy of starring as a gun-toting serial killer in the latest spate of loony brat movies, for which American society and for that matter the British too have an insatiable and never ending hunger? The eager eyes and rubbing palms of IFA who would be waiting to prey on their young saleable flesh.

As a young player he was no less devoted to his calling than a priest to the cloth. While not exactly a celibate, he had never formed deep relationships or procreated. In lonely and meditative moments he used the instability of his profession as his excuse and, anyway, wished nothing to interfere with his goal to be a servant of the classics. In the early days his light was seen to shine in some of the major reps drawing many admirers to his virile Petruchio, a demonic Macbeth, a poetic Richard II. But temptation to earn some money in long West End runs of thrillers reduced the glow somewhat, though, to speak true, lack of more classical opportunities made this temporary fall from grace necessary.

All this is meant to explain this devotee's lack of wife or family, who might have tugged at him, made demands of his love and energy, that would temper the single-minded and obsessive drive the gods demand before their gifts are bestowed. But he had to admit that his devotion was to a rather tough god who reminded him of his father and had, as yet, rewarded him with nothing – except isolation. Perhaps one carries the father's patterns like a tape within one, and in some inevitable way, constructs one's own rejection. Consequently it will be perceived that the agent's neglect of the simple dues of respectful behaviour that might have earned contempt in a healthy body, in Harry opened a wound a mile wide. Into it flew every doubt he ever had. He felt he was in a void. But, the one agent he had resisted would without doubt take him on his books, as he does eventually with everyone, for none shall escape him. Being methodical as behoves bachelor actors, Harry made his will, settled his affairs and then, in an act that had a touch of theatricality about it, calmly threw himself under a train at Leicester Square Tube.

PS. This was a tad uncharacteristically thoughtless of him and must have demonstrated the stress he was under for, had he known what chaos this was to cause on the Piccadilly Line that afternoon, his own natural and rather touching concern not to be the cause of others' discomfort would surely have led him to make a less dramatic exit.